D1517043

For current pricing information,
or to learn more about this or any Nextext title,
call us toll-free at **1-800-323-5435**
or visit our web site at www.nextext.com.

A HISTORICAL READER

The Great
Depression

nextext

Cover photograph: *A migrant mother and her daughter in front of their trailer home near Weslaco, Texas, February 1939.* Photograph by Russell Lee, courtesy of the Library of Congress.

Copyright © 2002 by McDougal Littell, a division of Houghton Mifflin Company. All rights reserved. Nextext® is an imprint of McDougal Littell.

No part of this work may be reproduced or transmitted in any form or by any means, electronic or mechanical, including photocopying and recording, or by any information storage or retrieval system without prior written permission of McDougal Littell unless such copying is expressly permitted by federal copyright law. With the exception of not-for-profit transcription in Braille, McDougal Littell is not authorized to grant permission for further uses of copyrighted selections reprinted in this text without the permission of their owners. Permission must be obtained from the individual copyright owners identified herein. Address inquiries to Manager, Rights and Permissions, McDougal Littell, P. O. Box 1667, Evanston, Illinois 60204.

Printed in the United States of America

ISBN 0-618-00367-3

5 6 7 8 9 10 — QVK — 06 05 04 03

Table of Contents

Throughout the reader, vocabulary words appear in boldface type and are footnoted. Specialized or technical words and phrases appear in lightface type and are footnoted.

Boom and Bust

chapter 4

Depressions Are Farm Led and Farm Fed

BY STUDS TERKEL

The Great Depression did not just happen suddenly the day the United States stock market crashed. Its beginnings were much earlier. For U. S. farmers, most of the 1920s was a very low period.

Studs Terkel, the noted journalist whose books of interviews with ordinary people have shed so much light on the twentieth century, wrote about the Depression in Hard Times: An Oral History of the Great Depression. *Here is a part of his interview with former South Dakota State Senator Emil Loriks, who served in the state legislature from 1927 through 1934. Loriks recalls the troubles at his family's farm in the early 1920s, how farmers fought back against the forced farm sales held when farmers couldn't pay their mortgages, and what it was like to represent farmers.*

In 1924, our grain elevator went broke. Farm prices collapsed. I remember signing a personal note, guaranteeing the commission company against loss. I didn't sleep very good those nights. The banks were failing all over the state. The squeeze was beginning to be felt. The stock market panic didn't come as any surprise to us. Our government had **systematically**[1] done everything wrong. . . . We were going to take the profits out of war. The only thing we did was put a ceiling on wheat. We passed high protective **tariffs,**[2] other countries **retaliated**[3]. . . .

There's a saying: "Depressions are farm led and farm fed." That was true in the Thirties. As farmers lost their purchasing power, the big tractors piled up at the Minneapolis-Moline plant in the Twin Cities. One day they closed their doors and turned their employees out to beg or starve. My cousin was one of them. I took my truck to Minneapolis and brought him and his family out to my farm for the duration. They stayed with us until the company opened up again, two or three years later.

During my first session in the state senate, in 1927, five hundred farmers came marching up Capitol Hill. It thrilled me. I didn't know farmers were intelligent enough to organize. (Laughs.) They stayed there for two days. It was a strength I didn't realize we had.

The day after they left, a Senator got up and attacked them as **anarchists**[4] and bolsheviks.[5] (Laughs.) They had a banner, he said, redder than anything in Moscow, Russia. What was this banner? It was a piece of muslin, hung up in the auditorium. It said: "We Buy Together, We Sell Together, We Vote Together." This was the radical danger. (Laughs.) They'd been building cooperatives, which the farmers badly needed.

---

[1] **systematically**—carried out in a thorough and methodical manner.

[2] **tariffs**—duties (fees) imposed by a government on imported or exported goods.

[3] **retaliated**—got even; paid back in kind.

[4] **anarchists**—people who believe in abolishing all forms of government.

[5] bolsheviks—those who engage in revolutionary or left-wing activities; Communists.

I was the first man to answer him from the senate floor. Eleven others took turns. He never got re-elected. In the lower house, we had about thirty or forty members of the Farmer's Union. It was quite an education for me. . . .

Oh, the **militancy**[6] then! At Milbank, during a farm sale, they had a sheriff and sixteen deputies. One of them got a little trigger-happy. It was a mistake. The boys disarmed him so fast he didn't know what happened. They just yanked the belts off 'em, didn't even unbuckle 'em. They took their guns away from 'em. After that, we didn't have much trouble stopping sales.

Thirteen highways to Sioux Falls were blocked. They emptied the stockyards there in a day or two. There was some violence, most of it accidental.

I'll never forget a speech by a Catholic priest at a Salem meeting, straight south of here about forty miles. It was the most fiery I ever heard. He said, "If you men haven't got the guts to picket the roads and stop this stuff from going to market, put on skirts and get in the kitchen and let your wives go out and do the job." (Laughs.) The boys used the police stations as their headquarters. (Laughs.) The police couldn't do much. The sheriffs and deputies just had to go along.

That judge situation in Iowa was a warning.[7] In Brown County, farmers would crowd into the courtroom, five or six hundred, and make it impossible for the officers to carry out the sales. (Laughs.)

Deputies would come along with whole fleets of trucks and guns. One lone farmer had planks across the road. They ordered him to remove them. They came out with guns. He said, "Go ahead and shoot, but there isn't one of you . . . getting out of here alive." There were

---

[6]**militancy**—relating to or characteristic of an army; aggressiveness.

[7] A group of farmers angry about a farm sale took a judge out into the country and threatened to hang him for refusing to help stop the sale.

about fifteen hundred farmers there in the woods. The trucks didn't get through. It was close in spirit to the American Revolution.

QUESTIONS TO CONSIDER

1. Why does Terkel expect readers to laugh at his story about the senator who called the farmers anarchists and bolsheviks?

2. How was the farmers' resistance close in spirit to the American Revolution?

3. In what sense was the Depression "farm led"?

4. In your opinion, how justified were the farmers in protesting the sale of their farms?

from

Investments Soared

THE NEW YORK TIMES CHRONICLE
OF AMERICAN LIFE

*In the 1920s, the stock market was not regulated as it is today.
Also, there was enormous optimism about the business outlook.
People hoped they could get very rich by investing in companies
and in trusts. They borrowed money to buy stocks, believing that
the stocks would become worth so much, they would be able
to pay back their loans with the profits. The following selection
describes the mood among stockholders and some of the
schemes that became their folly.*

By the beginning of 1928 speculating in the stock
market had become almost a national mania. It was not
true that "everybody" was "in the market," as was
commonly said at the time; it just seemed that way.
Actually, only about a million persons owned stocks on
margin in September 1929—chiefly the amateur and
professional speculators—and about two million owned
shares outright. But the mania, like the national obses-
sion with a seven-game World Series, had made most of

the citizenry **vicarious**[1] speculators. Next to crime, the most engrossing news on any day's front page was likely to be what had happened on the market: Radio up another 6⅜; bears rout bulls in raid on Anaconda; Cleveland's Van Sweringen brothers reported buying heavily to extend their rail empire; an unknown newcomer, Frisbee Consolidated, startles the analysts with a **meteoric**[2] rise, and so on. Nearly everyone could translate the **esoteric**[3] language of the financial specialists into the **patois**[4] of Main Street. Your barber or streetcar conductor was as emphatic in his expertise as your banker or lawyer. Enough people whom you knew, or knew of, were dabbling in the market to give **verisimilitude**[5] to the impression that everybody was doing it: a spinster aunt, a school principal, the clerk at the post office, the taxi driver, the typist in the office pool. Everyone was prepared to believe such stories as that of the banker's chauffeur who had held on to his fifty shares of something-or-other after the banker had dumped his, and cleaned up a cool $1,500. Exploits such as these were the talk of the town—any town—the stuff of exciting folklore.

To satisfy this urge for fast riches, brokerage offices **proliferated**[6] across the country, in cities, suburbs, and small towns, like recruiting stations in wartime. Most branch offices had direct wire connections with New York or other big city establishments, and bore the outward marks, at least, of respectability. Others consisted of no more than a battery of rented telephones installed in a vacant store or hotel suite, manned by a squad of

---

[1] **vicarious**—experienced or realized through imaginative participation in the experience of another.

[2] **meteoric**—resembling a meteor in speed or in sudden and temporary brilliance.

[3] **esoteric**—of or relating to knowledge that is restricted to a small group.

[4] **patois**—speech or dialect of a certain group of people.

[5] **verisimilitude**—the quality of appearing to be true or real; likelihood.

[6] **proliferated**—increased by rapid production.

confidence men who kept their packed suitcases handily by their sides. These "bucket shops" and "boiler factories," dealing in the shards of unlisted, unknown, and even nonexistent securities, differed from the starched-collar establishments mainly in that they offered their victims a faster, closer shearing.

To accommodate the timid and the **skeptical**,[7] there was a sharp revival of the investment trust in the late twenties. An investment trust was a company that owned nothing but the stock of other companies. An investor with as little as ten dollars could buy a share in the trust in the expectation that he would profit proportionately as the trust reaped dividends from its portfolio. He was assured of the additional advantage over the freelance speculator that the trust's operations were guided by Wall Street experts of great wisdom; there was usually an impressive roster of bankers, corporation executives, and financiers on the letterhead.

There were fewer than a hundred investment trusts in existence in 1926; by the summer of 1929 there were more than 500, with more than $3 billion worth of shares held by an unnumbered legion of principally small investors. It was usual practice for the organizers to cut themselves and their friends in for sizeable blocks of the new stock at less than the opening price. If the trust had prominent backing, as many of them did, an almost instantaneous rise in price was assured. Thus, in January 1929 J. P. Morgan and Company, the most impeccable name in high finance, launched an investment trust called United Corporation. The partners and their friends bought in at $75 a share in advance of the public offering. When the shares went on sale the price was $92; before the first week was out they had been bid up to $100.

---

[7] **skeptical**—doubtful, suspicious, or uncertain.

Inevitably, many of these trusts were tacked together on the shakiest of foundations, but it seemed not to matter. The public demand for their stock was **insatiable.**[8] In many instances the value of the shares offered exceeded by two or three times the total value of the stocks and other assets on which they were based.

New investment trusts were spawned by a process of inbreeding that almost guaranteed a sterile offspring. In the summer of 1929, for example, the New York financial house of Goldman, Sachs and Company floated the Shenandoah Corporation, a third of whose assets was stock in another investment trust, the Goldman Sachs Trading Corporation. Within a few weeks, the same company announced the creation of still another and larger trust, the Blue Ridge Corporation, 80 percent of whose capital consisted of stock in the Shenandoah Corporation. Thus one investment trust could be built atop another, and the people who bought nearly $250 million worth of stock in Shenandoah and Blue Ridge owned virtually nothing that represented real wealth: no factories, no airlines, no oil wells, nothing but a ticket in a lottery. There were few laws in 1929 about how the sucker trap could be baited.

The dazzling pace of the investment splurge was not without its Cassandras.[9] "It is perfectly well recognized by 'insiders,'" the *Journal of Commerce* observed late in 1928, "that a market of the kind that has been going on cannot last indefinitely but must undergo a readjustment." Possibly the "insiders" did know it, but few of them, even those in positions of responsibility in government, wanted the unpleasant task of saying so. Secretary of the Treasury Andrew W. Mellon was no man to spread the alarm; he and his family had profited handsomely in the great bull market. President Hoover

---

[8] **insatiable**—incapable of being satisfied.

[9] Cassandras—people who predict misfortune or disaster.

could not bring himself to rock the boat, although he confessed years later in his published *Memoirs* that he realized it was sailing in perilous waters. When the Federal Reserve Board issued a cautious and **ambiguous**[10] warning that speculation was approaching the danger point, Arthur Brisbane, the widely read Hearst columnist, reproached it scornfully: "If buying and selling stocks is wrong, the government should close the Stock Exchange. If not, the Federal Reserve should mind its own business."

Up and up the market soared, gaining speed and spinning off miracles as it went. Between 1928 and 1929 the value of new capital issues offered jumped from $9.9 to $11.6 billion. Between June and the end of August of the latter year there was a gain of an unprecedented 110 registered on *The New York Times* average of 25 industrials, reaching an all-time high of 449 on September 3. To better illustrate what this meant, here are the gains made by a few blue-chip issues in the eighteen months between March 3, 1928, when many thought mistakenly the peak had been reached, and September 3, 1929, when the peak actually was reached: American Can, 77 to 181; American Telephone and Telegraph, 179 to 335; General Electric, 128 to 396; Montgomery Ward, 132 to 466; Radio Corporation of America, 94 to 505; United States Steel, 138 to 279; Electric Bond and Share, 89 to 203.

---

[10] **ambiguous**—doubtful or uncertain because of multiple interpretations.

QUESTIONS TO CONSIDER

1. Why does the author compare an investment in trusts, such as the Shenandoah, to a lottery ticket?

2. If the government officials knew that the stock market was heading for danger, why didn't they take action to prevent it?

3. What kinds of laws would you enact to protect unsuspecting investors from the traps of confidence men?

October 24, 1929

BY EDWARD ROBB ELLIS

Individuals with savings and corporations with surpluses began buying common stocks in 1924. By January 1, 1926, President Hoover began to worry about the prospect of speculation and inflation. By 1927, speculation began in earnest. That year, there were 290 millionaires in the United States. By 1929, there were 511. Stock market news was big news, and it occupied the front pages of all the major newspapers. Throughout this period, stock prices rose and some fell. The market reached its peak on September 3, 1929. Throughout the next six weeks, prices fell steadily, although some individual stocks stayed strong. However, on October 24, 1929, the market itself crashed.

On Thursday, October 24, 1929, the *New York Times* reported the previous day's trading in a front-page two-column headline that said:

PRICES OF STOCKS CRASH IN HEAVY
LIQUIDATION; TOTAL DROP OF BILLIONS

The *Times* and other morning papers published Washington dispatches quoting treasury officials as saying that the market break had been due to speculation[1] and did not represent any basic weakness in American business.

It was a cloudy day with the temperature in the low 50's and a light wind blowing from the northwest, so brokers and bankers wore topcoats to work. At 9:45 A.M. on the dot, as he did each business day, Otto Kahn stepped out of a limousine in front of his office at 52 William Street, one block east of the exchange. Kahn was senior partner of the renowned banking firm of Kuhn, Loeb & Company. Some said he had the slowest gait and the quickest mind in New York. Still a dandy at the age of sixty-two, Kahn was a handsome man with white hair, a gray waxed mustache and intense dark eyes. He wore an English-tailored suit, stiff collar, gray spats,[2] a carefully folded handkerchief peeping from his breast pocket, and a fresh boutonniere[3] in his lapel. The faint calm smile on his face was somehow comforting to sallow red-eyed brokers who had slept little and now dreaded the day ahead.

When the clock on the west wall of the trading room struck ten, Superintendent William B. Crawford hit the gong to signal the opening of trading. Brokers rushed toward the posts clutching handfuls of customers' orders. Orders to sell. After holding firm for a few minutes, most stocks began declining. The securities were not sold in small lots but in huge blocks; they were being dumped into the market. Six thousand shares of Montgomery Ward sold at 83 points; earlier in the year this stock went for 156. Twenty thousand shares of Kennecott Copper were sold. So enormous was the volume of trading that by 10:30 A.M. the ticker[4] was

---

[1] speculation—the buying or selling of stocks in expectation of profiting from changes in the market.

[2] spats—ankle-high shoes.

[3] boutonniere—a flower worn in one's buttonhole.

[4] ticker—a machine that automatically prints stock prices on a long strip of paper.

fifteen minutes behind. This lag was confusing, for spreads of up to 30 points developed between prices quoted on the floor and those recorded on the tardy tape.

By 11 A.M. all was panic. Prices were plunging 5, 10, even 15 points a minute. It seemed that everyone was scrambling to sell at whatever price he could get. On this spectacular day 1,100 brokers and 1,000 assistants thronged the trading floor and clustered about the trading posts, shouting and signaling. They were doing their best to handle the thousands upon thousands of selling orders that poured into Wall Street. Brokers feverishly made long-distance calls the length and breadth of America to demand margin,[5] more margin, from their customers.

By this date the Marx Brothers had taken their show *Animal Crackers* to Baltimore, and during the morning a telephone call awakened Groucho Marx in his Baltimore hotel room. It was his broker.

"Sorry to disturb you," said the broker, "but there's been a little slump in the market and I'll have to ask you for more margin."

Groucho, who thought he was worth $240,000 in securities, asked in disbelief: "Margin? What kind of a slump *is* it? I thought I had everything covered so nothing could touch it."

"Well-ll-l," the broker replied, "it's sort of a . . . a crisis . . . . I don't know how much longer I can hold out."

The same bad news was radioed to the Cunard liner *Berengaria,* a day's run east of New York on a return voyage from England. She carried 1,414 passengers, many of whom had been playing the stock market. They now jammed the brokerage office set up on shipboard by Michael J. Meehan, and those unable to edge inside

---

[5] margin—cash or assets that are deposited with a stockbroker to cover the difference between the price of the stock and the amount the investor has paid for it.

stood dejectedly just outside the door. The ones inside and up front watched the flying fingers of the board boy as he chalked the latest quotation on a blackboard. One trembling woman lost $160,000 in the first few hours of trading; later she recovered all but $40,000 of this sum. These shipboard passengers, so far from the center of action, traded almost 20,000 shares of stocks—with most of them losing.

City editors of New York newspapers pulled reporters and feature writers off routine assignments and sent them running toward Wall Street. One, a reporter for the United Press, was a thin-faced young man who had just moved to the big city, had only $10 to his name and knew nothing at all about financial news. He was told to go to an office at 111 Broadway, interview an important banker named Frank Vanderlip and find out what the whole thing meant. The reporter's name was H. Allen Smith, and in years to come he won fame as a humorist; but on this October 24, 1929, he saw nothing funny about his responsibility in reporting a crisis. Vanderlip, who took pity on Smith's ignorance, told him: "The fact of the matter is that I don't know what it means, either, my friends don't know what it means, and probably nobody knows what it means."

With **bedlam**[6] developing inside the exchange and crowds gathering on the streets outside, Police Commissioner Grover Whalen decided to send police reinforcements to the scene. In the previous few days 60 detectives and 50 uniformed cops had been stationed in and around Wall Street. Whalen now dispatched an extra 100 detectives, 400 patrolmen and a detail of mounted men.

As newsreelmen set up their cameras at strategic points near the exchange, throngs before its doors swapped wild rumors. Word was passed that the Chicago

---

[6] **bedlam**—a scene or state of uproar and confusion.

and Buffalo exchanges had closed—which was untrue. Eleven big speculators were supposed to have killed themselves. When a repairman appeared on the high roof of a nearby building, people on the pavement murmured that he had lost a fortune and was about to jump. Ambulances were reported en route to other buildings where men **allegedly**[7] had shot themselves. Sightseeing buses abandoned their scheduled routes and detoured to Wall Street to see the excitement.

By 11:30 A.M., with the ticker forty-eight minutes behind, hysteria gripped the traders on the exchange floor, and panic rolled in waves from New York to California. The crisis was beyond belief. Twenty thousand shares of Du Pont stock were dumped on the market, but there was no bid. Minute after tingling minute not a single sale was made. Nobody wanted to buy. Everybody wanted to sell, sell, sell. Only after certain stocks fell to ridiculously low prices did some daring men purchase them.

At 12 noon reporters saw three prominent bankers enter J. P. Morgan's private bank at 23 Wall Street, just across the street from the exchange. They were Charles E. Mitchell, chairman of the National City Bank; Albert H. Wiggin, chairman of the Chase National Bank; and William Potter, president of the Guaranty Trust Company. Sidewalk gawkers did not recognize these men, but reporters shouted their names and titles to one another.

Morgan's bank was a squat, five-story gray building worth nearly $6 million—double the cost of the main building of the New York Stock Exchange. With the great Morgan himself vacationing in Great Britain, the other bankers had been summoned by the senior Morgan partner, Thomas Lamont. Already present inside the bank was Seward Prosser, chairman of the Morgan firm, and the group was later joined by George

---

[7] **allegedly**—supposedly; thought to be true, but without proof.

F. Baker, Jr., chairman of the First National Bank of New York. Bernard Baruch had been invited to attend this meeting, but he stayed away because he thought he smelled a rat.

The emergency meeting of these influential bankers was called to order by Lamont in his small private office on the second floor of the Morgan bank. One of the most powerful men in the United States, Thomas W. Lamont at the age of fifty-nine was a renowned international banker, spokesman for the Morgan firm, diplomat, writer, editor, publisher, politician and statesman who was often consulted by Presidents, prime ministers and governors of European central banks. He was short and slender, slightly stooped, with gray hair. He did not always mask his emotions, as did many bankers, but had a highly expressive face. At all times he was charming and courteous.

Lamont now sat at the antique Italian table that served as his desk. The walls of his office were paneled in dark oak, and the north wall, overlooking Wall Street, was pierced by two windows containing small transparencies of the glass in Chartres Cathedral. Above the fireplace hung an oil painting of the 1813 engagement between the *Chesapeake* and the *Shannon;* only a little while before this critical day Lamont had paid $400,000 for another precious painting.

After he greeted his fellow bankers, who took their places in high-backed, carved and uncomfortable chairs, the first thing Lamont did was to telephone the White House and ask President Hoover to issue a reassuring statement. This was an ironic reversal of roles. Earlier in the year, when Hoover sent a personal emissary to Wall Street to ask the bankers to admit that the market was unsound, Lamont had rejected the President's appeal. Hoover later wrote in his memoirs that "Thomas Lamont of Morgan's wrote me a long memorandum which makes curious reading today."

Aware of the sickening crisis on the floor of the exchange, the six bankers decided to form a **coalition**[8] to pump new life into the dying market. This they did by forming a pool, with each pledging $40 million for a total of $240 million. An additional $100 million was supplied by other financial firms, including the Guggenheim Brothers and James Speyer and Company. It was by far the largest concentration of pool buying power ever directed at the stock market. The bankers did not seek to establish any particular price level in the market. What they wanted to do was to indulge in a bold psychological gesture to end the panic—and protect themselves.

This strategy was agreed on in a mere twenty minutes. The bankers understood that to make a success of this pool, unlike other pools, they needed all the publicity they could get. As the other grim-faced financiers hurried back to their own offices, Lamont walked down one flight to the lobby of the Morgan bank, where he faced reporters. His expression serious, but his voice calm, Lamont announced to the press that "there has been a little distress selling on the Stock Exchange." This understatement has since become a Wall Street classic. Distress selling means a feverish wish to sell at any price. However, Lamont continued, this selling was "due to a technical condition of the market," rather than to any fundamental trouble. He was sure that things were "susceptible to betterment."

During the morning the **frenetic**[9] action on the floor of the exchange drew 722 sightseers to the visitors' gallery, where their excited cries added to the deafening noise in the big room. At 12:30 P.M. these people were ushered out, and the gallery was closed. Among those who had been watching was a visiting Englishman,

---

[8] **coalition**—a temporary alliance formed for the purpose of taking action.
[9] **frenetic**—frenzied; frantic.

Winston Churchill, who recently had resigned as Great Britain's chancellor of the exchequer.[10]

By 1 P.M., with the ticker now ninety-two minutes behind, stock values had shrunk a total of about $11 billion, and the newly formed bankers' pool was about to swing into action. E. H. H. Simmons, the president of the New York Stock Exchange, was far away in Hawaii on his honeymoon. In his absence, Lamont and the other bankers had chosen the vice-president, Richard Whitney, to make their move. Whitney was about to have his hour of glory.

At 1:15 P.M. he sauntered out onto the floor. Because Whitney was seldom seen there, because word of the bankers' emergency meeting had seeped into the exchange and because everyone could guess his mission, brokers gasped when they saw him. **Debonair,**[11] almost jaunty, Whitney shouldered his way through the masses of men and up to trading post No. 2, where United States Steel was sold. When trading had begun in the morning, Steel had started at 205 ½, a point or two above the previous day's closing. During the day it sank to a low of 193 ½, and minutes before Whitney's appearance it had been hovering around 195.

In a loud and confident voice, Whitney now offered to buy 25,000 shares of Steel at 205—or 10 points *above* the asking price. This *beau geste,* this expression of confidence in the market, was so heartening to brokers that they burst into cheers. Order clerks shouted the electrifying news through direct-wire telephones to every brokerage house in New York, and within seconds it was relayed to every corner of the nation. The big bankers had made their move. They were protecting the market. The longed-for organized support had come to the rescue in the nick of time.

---

[10] chancellor of the exchequer—member of the British cabinet in charge of public money.

[11] **debonair**—unconcerned, lighthearted.

Then and there, Whitney bought 200 shares of United States Steel, leaving the balance of his order with a specialist—an exchange member who executes orders given him by other brokers. With all eyes following him, Whitney then moved on to other trading posts, purchasing other stocks in blocks of 10,000 and 20,000 shares. Inside half an hour he bought 200,000 shares of various securities at a cost to the bankers' pool of more than $20 million.

By 2 P.M. the market had taken a vigorous upward turn. Although some selling continued, Whitney's grandstand play seemed to have stemmed the panic. Stock prices rallied. General Electric, for example, bounced back 25 points. At the end of the day's trading, United States Steel closed at 206.

At 3 P.M., with the ringing of the gong, trading ended. Brokers leaned wearily against trading posts, their collars torn, their faces wet with sweat. A record-breaking total of 12,894,650 shares had been traded, and the industrial average was down a little more than 12 points. The ticker had fallen so far behind transactions that it did not stop chattering until 7:08 P.M., more than four hours after the exchange closed for the day.

Only then could the magnitude of the disaster be calculated. All day long the exchange's telephone system had been clogged with calls from speculators eager to learn where they stood. Thousands of small investors now heard that they had been wiped out. In one small community in upper New York State 108 of 150 families had been playing the market on margin; now only 6 of these families had any securities left. Thousands of brokerage and bank accounts, prosperous a mere week earlier, had been wrecked.

Elliott V. Bell, a young financial writer for the *New York Times*, dropped in to see a vice-president of one of the larger banks in New York. The financier was walking back and forth in his office. Looking up, he said: "Well, Elliott, I thought I was a millionaire a few days ago. Now I find I'm looking through the wrong end of the telescope." Laughing bitterly, he added: "We'll get those bastards that did this yet!" The reporter never did find out what "bastards" he meant but later learned that the vice-president was not merely broke but hopelessly in debt.

In Washington a furious Senator Carter Glass snarled: "The present trouble is due largely to Charles E. Mitchell's[12] activities! That man—more than forty others—is responsible for the present situation. Had the Federal Reserve acted and dismissed him, the trouble might be less. The crash has shown that stock gambling has reached its limit."

In New York, Mitchell himself commented: "This reaction has badly outrun itself."

In London, British economist John Maynard Keynes declared that the market break would benefit the world because it would **liquidate**[13] unsound speculation. Keynes argued that credit which had been absorbed by the market now would be freed for the use of industry, and commodity prices would recover.

But this was theory. Reality, crushing reality, had broken over the heads of thousands upon thousands of Americans, who stared at tickers in their brokers' offices until the end of the business day, then slumped in chairs, their faces gray, too stunned and exhausted to get to their feet to stagger home. On Wall Street itself, lights blazed in windows of tall office buildings as over-worked clerks and bookkeepers pawed their way through mountains of papers in an effort to catch up with the day's transactions. Hundreds of thousands of shares of stock also had to be earmarked for sale the next day. The workers fainted at their desks. Runners

---

[12] Charles E. Mitchell was the chairman of the National City Bank.

[13] **liquidate**—to settle by payment.

fell exhausted on the marble floors of banks and slept. Others, like fellow passengers on a sinking ship, indulged in a kind of frenetic gaiety of despair. Some messengers and boardroom boys, high on excitement they understood only dimly, frolicked along the sidewalks until cops were called to quiet them. The boys were given short and stern lectures: This was no Roman holiday but a national disaster! Hadn't they heard the news from Seattle about the secretary of a finance company who had shot himself to death?

QUESTIONS TO CONSIDER

1. What was unusual or different about the trading done on October 24, 1929?

2. What was the purpose of the action taken by the bankers who met that day in Thomas Lamont's office?

3. Describe in your own words what the bank vice-president meant when he said after the crash: "I thought I was a millionaire a few days ago. Now I find I'm looking through the wrong end of the telescope."

Ed Uhl, Bank Loan Officer, and Marty Ducceschi, Depositor

BY TOM SHACHTMAN

Playwright and documentary filmmaker Tom Shachtman wrote an hour-by-hour account of October 24 in his book The Day America Crashed. *Using the personal recollections of hundreds of individuals, he reconstructed the events of that fateful day as they affected the rich and powerful bankers and brokers of Wall Street, the small investors and businessmen, the farmers, and the multitude of white- and blue-collar workers across the country. This selection looks at banks and loans from two different perspectives. Ed Uhl spent the day calling in the margin accounts. Marty Ducceschi remembers an earlier time when the bank closed and his family lost its farm as well as each other's good will.*

Ed Uhl, in charge of the loan department in a downtown Philadelphia bank, knew it would be a long day. Margin calls were his unpleasant business. Everyone including the bootblack[1] in their building seemed to be in the market, getting tips from the brokers in the area, spreading the word about the possibility of a rise in this or that stock, or a split-up in another. Ed could never understand why when a stock split it seemed that the two half-shares were worth more than a full share. But these were the days of the bulls.[2] The only bear[3] he ever came across was in the zoo. In the meantime, shifting prices meant a tremendous load of work for his loan department, which had much money out that was secured by stocks as collateral.[4] In many banks across the country, the unsettled market that had existed since Labor Day had caused loan officers to reconsider their margin requirements daily. High-flying stocks were discounted many points, and then margin was computed for each account. Margins were generally at 25 percent, except for these high-flying stocks. Since Labor Day cautious bankers had been pushing them up to 35 and even to 50 percent. But the situation was changing every day, and loans, as well as loan officers, had to be flexible. You didn't want to lose a customer by raising the margin too high, but at the same time you didn't want the bank to lose money if the market fell sharply, more sharply than had been anticipated. So, of late, the routine had been that after the bank and the markets had closed, Ed's people would be there until nine, ten, eleven o'clock before going home, making their notes on the loan cards. These they did with the aid of the evening newspapers with the closing prices. Each night the collateral on each card was repriced and retotaled, the margin was computed, and, if it was inadequate, the card was set

---

[1] bootblack—someone who shines shoes.

[2] bulls—investors who buy into the stock market in the expectation that the price of stocks will go up.

[3] bear—investor who sells stocks in the expectation that stock prices will go down.

[4] collateral—money or property pledged to back up a loan.

aside to be reviewed by three officers, who would decide on what kind of a letter was to be sent to a borrower.

Letter number 1 was a notice that margin was impaired, please deposit additional collateral or cash. There was no time limit on these letters, but most people came the next day and put up what was needed. In case they didn't, the next day they'd be sent letter number 2, which told them to come in as soon as possible the next day. Most of the people with loans were depositors in the bank; they usually reduced the loan with their money on deposit if additional collateral was not available. All of the loans were payable on demand. If a borrower's loan of $1,000 was secured by shares worth $1,250, when the value of the stocks had dropped to, say, $1,100, the bank would request additional collateral worth $150 or its equivalent in cash. If the borrower had enough cash or collateral to keep up the loan to the required amount, after letters 1 and 2, fine. If not, he got letter number 3. Inside the bank, this was known as a "hereby do." Sent by special delivery, it stated that it was necessary to call the loan for payment at a certain hour the next day, which we "hereby do." The letter had been composed by the bank's lawyers and further said that all collateral would be sold by the bank if the demand was not met. Even though there might be an excess if everything a borrower held as collateral were sold, the bank couldn't very well sell selectively, and would possibly have been subject to a borrower's suit if they didn't protect him from a greater loss, say if the market continued to fall.

For the first time in a while there had been a fair number of "hereby do" letters in the batch sent out last night. In another three hours, those people ought to show up and pay on their loans, or Ed would have to go through the unpleasant task of selling their securities.

As yesterday's market had been unsettled, this was a distinct possibility for today.

Marty Ducceschi, working at the throwing mill on Gray Street in Paterson, New Jersey, had mixed thoughts about banks, loans, and everything that had to do with the dream house of his childhood. In 1927, when he was fifteen, the house and the 160-acre farm in Donora, Pennsylvania, near the Monongahela River, had seemed paradise. They had some cows and pigs, a nice house, barrels outside to catch the rainwater which was soft and good for washing clothes. His older brother worked in a blast furnace at a nearby steel mill, and Marty thought he might do that someday as well, and possibly play soccer for the Gallatin town team, which was one of the best in an area filled with many good ones. On nice days they'd drive over to Uniontown and see some of the beautiful mansions put up by the people who owned the steel and zinc mills and the coal mines. Marty had also witnessed at Uniontown his first coal miner's strike and an explosion, neither of them pretty sights. Nearly every night, at the farm, Marty's family and his uncle's family would get together. The men were brothers. They'd play cards and drink homemade wine or beer in the front, while the women would talk and knit or darn socks in the kitchen, and the cousins would all play games. It was lots of fun. But then things changed.

Marty's uncle had, somehow, gotten inside information that the Donora bank was going to close and withdrew his money in time. Throughout the twenties, nearly a thousand banks had closed all over the country, usually small state banks in rural areas. The depression of 1920–1921, which for farmers had lengthened to include most of the decade of the twenties, had taken its toll on these small state banks which were not under federal control and had no guarantees for depositors. As the loans to farmers were **defaulted**,[5] and those to the city dwellers who serviced the farmers caved in soon thereafter, whole areas were deeply affected with financial **blight**.[6] In some states as many as 43 percent of the banks had closed, and no state was **immune**[7] from the disease. Putting your money in a state bank was not the safest thing in world, as people were finding out to their **chagrin**.[8] Here, the people of the Monongahela Valley were affected in Donora, Webster, Charleroi, Monessen, New Eagle, Gallatin, Cement City, Uniontown, Turkey Hollows, Monongahela, and Black Diamond.

For some reason, Marty's uncle hadn't told his brother of the coming closing, and it hit Marty's family hard. With many others, they joined the crowds around the bank's doors, trying to get at their life's savings, but to no avail. They lost the farm. Father was bitter at his brother for not having told him of the bank's impending close. Then—the worst thing!—Marty's uncle purchased the farm from the bank's receivers and moved his family in where Marty's had once been. This occasioned a blood feud. No one talked to a member of the opposite **faction**.[9] The cousins grew apart. One night Marty's father had gone and smashed the rain barrels at the old place in a hopeless gesture of anger.

At last they all piled into the old Ford and headed for New Jersey. Marty's job at the mill helped, now: it brought ten dollars a week.

---

[5] **defaulted**—failed to pay or make good.

[6] **blight**—an impaired or decayed condition.

[7] **immune**—exempt from; not susceptible to.

[8] **chagrin**—a feeling of embarrassment or humiliation caused by failure or disappointment.

[9] **faction**—small group forming a cohesive minority within and usually against a larger group.

QUESTIONS TO CONSIDER

1. Of the three letters Ed Uhl had to send to bank customers, which one carried the heaviest penalty? Why?

2. What caused the blood feud between Marty and his uncle?

3. Do you think the uncle was right to buy Marty's family farm? Why or why not?

4. Why do you think the author included Ed's and Marty's stories in the same article?

What Caused the Crash?

BY EDWARD ROBB ELLIS

*Most major historic events have multiple causes and are further
complicated by human motives. The Depression was no exception.
Here Ellis relates explanations from such figures as the financier
J. P. Morgan, Presidents Coolidge and Hoover, and the plainspoken
governor of Louisiana, Huey Long.*

People laughed when they read in their newspapers
of November 7, 1929, about a New York cop who found
an escaped parrot shuffling along Fifth Avenue at
Eighty-first Street. The parrot was squawking: "More
margin! More margin!"

But people did not laugh very long. They wanted an
answer to one overriding question: What caused the
Crash on Wall Street?

At the time of the Crash, soon thereafter and even
down to the present day a variety of explanations were
offered to the public. There is nothing surprising about

this diversity of opinions. Economics is not an exact science. Stock market operations cannot be reduced to one simple mathematical formula. Whenever J. Pierpont Morgan had been asked what he thought the market would do, he always replied: "It will **fluctuate.**"[1] This was no wisecrack. Morgan never indulged in wisecracks. He simply described the market's essential trait: It goes up and it goes down. Now, in 1929, it had gone down so fast and far that everyone was bewildered. When they were able to collect their thoughts, when they tried to comprehend this complex and massive event, each saw it through the prism of his own personality and experience.

Calvin Coolidge may have suffered personal **remorse**[2] but he was not willing to accept public blame. In an article written for the *Saturday Evening Post* the former President listed a variety of factors, then said: ". . . It will be observed that all these causes of depression, with the exception of the early speculation,[3] had their origin outside of the United States, where they were entirely beyond the control of our Government."

President Herbert Hoover offered several explanations of the Crash and the following Depression.

He declared that "our immediate weak spot was the orgy of stock speculation which began to slump in October, 1929." As for speculators themselves, Hoover added that "there are crimes far worse than murder for which men should be **reviled**[4] and punished." But a second cause, according to the President, was World War I and its aftereffects. Hoover's war hypothesis was publicly attacked by Senator Carter Glass, who growled that the Depression was no more caused by World War I

---

[1] **fluctuate**—to be changing constantly and irregularly.

[2] **remorse**—a deep regret arising from a sense of guilt for past wrongs.

[3] speculation—the buying or selling of stocks in expectation of profiting from changes in the market.

[4] **reviled**—subjected to verbal abuse.

than it was by the "war of the Phoenicians or the conquest of Gaul by Caesar." It was also criticized in private by Harlan F. Stone, then an Associate Justice of the United States Supreme Court and later its Chief Justice.

Hoover then fell back on Coolidge's argument that the chief causes of the Crash and Depression lay outside the United States. This did not square, however, with findings of the **impartial**[5] Brookings Institution of Washington, D.C., after its experts had studied conditions in twenty-seven nations, including the United States. According to their report, before prosperity ended in the United States, it had been terminated in eight other nations—Canada, Argentina, Brazil, Germany, Finland, Poland, Australia and the Netherlands Indies. The United States entered the Depression at just about the same time as three other nations—Belgium, Italy and Egypt. However, the United States plunged into the Depression *earlier* than fifteen other nations—Great Britain, Switzerland, Holland, Austria, Czechoslovakia, France, Denmark, Norway, Ireland, Yugoslavia, Japan, India, British Malaya, New Zealand and South Africa. . . .

Governor Huey Long of Louisiana said much the same thing in plain words: "The wealth of the land was being tied up in the hands of a very few men. The people were not buying because they had nothing with which to buy. The big business interests were not selling, because there was nobody they could sell to. One percent of the people could not eat any more than any other one percent; they could not wear much more than any other one percent; they could not live in any more houses than any other one percent. So, in 1929, when the fortune-holders of America grew powerful enough that one percent of the people owned nearly everything, ninety-nine percent of the people owned practically nothing, not even enough to pay their debts, a collapse was at hand. . . ."

---

[5]**impartial**—unbiased, fair.

What caused the Crash?

Greedy people wanted more than they needed. Foolish people thought they could get something for nothing. Impulsive people bought now in the hope of paying later. Income and wealth were distributed unfairly and dangerously. The rich regarded themselves as an all-knowing **elite**.[6] The masses were not paid enough money to consume all the goods they produced. The economy was unsound. The corporate structure was sick. The banking system was weak. Foreign trade was out of balance. Business data were inadequate and often faulty.

This **constellation**[7] of conditions left the economy a flawed and loaded gun, and when the stock market crashed, the gun did not merely fire—it exploded in everyone's face.

---

[6] **elite**—a socially superior group.

[7] **constellation**—a set of objects, properties, or individuals, especially a structurally related grouping.

QUESTIONS TO CONSIDER

1. How were the diverse interpretations of the stock market crash influenced by people's personality and experience?

2. On what grounds did the Brookings Institution challenge Coolidge's argument that the crash and the Depression were caused by forces outside the U.S.?

3. Does the author agree with Governor Huey Long's theory about the crash? Why or why not?

4. In what ways was the U.S. economy a flawed and loaded gun in 1929?

The Crash

Sleepless Nights The crash wiped out family savings and with them plans for the future.

Hoovervilles President Hoover was widely blamed for the situation. The ramshackle camps in which homeless people lived became known as "Hoovervilles."
▼

Living in Squalor People made homes out of anything they could find, and living conditions for children and families were desperate.

▲

It's Over On December 26, the cover of *Life* magazine characterized the year. Nineteen twenty-nine is stuffed in a trash can in front of a stock ticker-tape machine, while rolls of worthless tape curl up like wisps of smoke.

Worshiping a False God On its November 13, 1929, cover, *Life* magazine portrayed a crowd on Wall Street worshiping the golden calf, a reference to the Bible story in which Moses comes down from the mountain to find the mob worshiping a false god. ▶

WASHINGTON

THE GOLDEN CALF

SUB TR

Down on
Their Luck

"Brother, Can You Spare A Dime?"

SONG BY E.Y. (YIP) HARBURG

During the Depression years, songs expressed the mood of the country. "Brother, Can You Spare a Dime?" is probably the most famous song of the Depression era. Written by Yip Harburg, it expresses the disillusionment, sorrow, and shame of all who could not make it on their own.

They used to tell me I was building a dream,
And so I followed the mob—
When there was earth to plough or guns to bear
I was always there—right there on the job.
They used to tell me I was building a dream
With peace and glory ahead—
Why should I be standing in line
Just waiting for bread?

REFRAIN:

Once I built a railroad, made it run,
Made it race against time.
Once I built a railroad,
Now it's done—
Brother, can you spare a dime?
Once I built a tower, to the sun.
Brick and **rivet**[1] *and lime,*
Once I built a tower,
Now it's done—
Brother, can you spare a dime?
Once in khaki suits,
Gee, we looked swell,
Full of that Yankee Doodle-de-dum.
Half a million boots went sloggin' thru Hell,[2]
I was the kid with the drum.
Say don't you remember, they called me Al—
It was Al all the time.
Say, don't you remember I'm your pal—
Buddy, can you spare a dime?

---

[1] **rivet**—a single-headed pin or bit of metal used for uniting two or more pieces.

[2] Harburg is referring to the troops who fought in World War I.

QUESTIONS TO CONSIDER

1. Why do you think this song became popular among Americans who lived through the Depression?

2. What special significance do you see in the terms "brother" and "buddy"?

3. Why do you think the song makes references to World War I?

Interview with E.Y. (Yip) Harburg

BY STUDS TERKEL

Yip Harburg was a songwriter who stayed employed throughout the Depression. While many were out of work, many others were not. In this interview, Harburg tells Studs Terkel how he felt freed by the Depression. He speaks about songwriting and, in particular, about "Brother, Can You Spare a Dime?"

I never liked the idea of living on scallions in a left bank **garret**.[1] I like writing in comfort. So I went into business, a classmate and I. I thought I'd retire in a year or two. And a thing called Collapse, bango! socked everything out. 1929. All I had left was a pencil.

Luckily, I had a friend named Ira Gershwin, and he said to me: "You've got your pencil. Get your rhyming dictionary and go to work." I did. There was nothing else to do. I was doing light verse at the time, writing a

---

[1] **garret**—attic room.

poem here and there for ten bucks a crack. It was an era when kids at college were interested in light verse and ballads and sonnets. This is the early Thirties.

I was relieved when the Crash came. I was released. Being in business was something I detested. When I found that I could sell a song or a poem, I became me, I became alive. Other people didn't see it that way. They were throwing themselves out of windows.

Someone who lost money found that his life was gone. When I lost my possessions, I found my creativity. I felt I was being born for the first time. So for me the world became beautiful.

With the Crash, I realized that the greatest fantasy of all was business. The only realistic way of making a living was versifying. Living off your imagination.

We thought American business was the Rock of Gibraltar. We were the prosperous nation, and nothing could stop us now. A brownstone house was forever. You gave it to your kids and they put marble fronts on it. There was a feeling of continuity. If you made it, it was there forever. Suddenly the big dream exploded. The impact was unbelievable.

I was walking along the street at that time, and you'd see the bread lines. The biggest one in New York City was owned by William Randolph Hearst. He had a big truck with several people on it, and big cauldrons of hot soup, bread. Fellows with burlap on their shoes were lined up all around Columbus Circle, and went for blocks and blocks around the park, waiting.

There was a skit in one of the first shows I did, *Americana*. This was 1930. In the sketch, Mrs. Ogden Reid of the *Herald Tribune* was very jealous of Hearst's beautiful bread line. It was bigger than her bread line. It was a **satiric,**[2] **volatile**[3] show. We needed a song for it.

---

[2] **satiric**—using biting wit, irony, or sarcasm to expose and discredit vice or folly.

[3] **volatile**—subject to sudden change.

On stage, we had men in old soldiers' uniforms, **dilapidated,**[4] waiting around. And then into the song. We had to have a title. And how do you do a song so it isn't **maudlin?**[5] Not to say: my wife is sick, I've got six children, the Crash put me out of business, hand me a dime. I hate songs of that kind. I hate songs that are on the nose. I don't like songs that describe a historic moment pitifully.

The prevailing greeting at that time, on every block you passed, by some poor guy coming up, was: "Can you spare a dime?" Or: "Can you spare something for a cup of coffee?" . . . "Brother, Can You Spare a Dime?" finally hit on every block, on every street. I thought that could be a beautiful title. If I could only work it out by telling people, through the song, it isn't just a man asking for a dime.

This is the man who says: I built the railroads. I built that tower. I fought your wars. I was the kid with the drum. Why the hell should I be standing in line now? What happened to all this wealth I created?

I think that's what made the song. Of course, together with the idea and meaning, a song must have poetry. It must have the phrase that rings a bell. The art of song writing is a craft. Yet, "Brother, Can You Spare a Dime?" opens up a political question. Why should this man be penniless at any time in his life, due to some fantastic thing called a Depression or sickness or whatever it is that makes him so insecure?

In the song the man is really saying: I made an investment in this country. Where the hell are my dividends? Is it a dividend to say: "Can you spare a dime?" What the hell is wrong? Let's examine this thing. It's more than just a bit of **pathos.**[6] It doesn't reduce him to

---

[4] **dilapidated**—partly ruined or decayed.

[5] **maudlin**—excessively sentimental.

[6] **pathos**—that which arouses pity or compassion.

a beggar. It makes him a dignified human, asking questions—and a bit outraged, too, as he should be.

Everybody picked the song up in '30 and '31. Bands were playing it and records were made. When Roosevelt was a candidate for President, the Republicans got pretty worried about it. Some of the network radio people were told to lay low on the song. In some cases, they tried to ban it from the air. But it was too late. The song had already done its damage.

QUESTIONS TO CONSIDER

1. Why was Mr. Harburg relieved when the Crash came?

2. Why do you think Mr. Harburg said that asking for a dime during the Depression made one a "dignified human being" rather than a beggar?

3. How did the Crash influence Americans' attitude toward business?

Bonus Army March on Washington

BY JOHN DOS PASSOS

In 1932, thousands of World War I veterans and their families marched on Washington to demand the passage of a bill that called for immediate payment of the bonuses they were due to receive in 1945. They were suffering from the Depression and believed that this was something their government could do to provide relief without charity. They had, after all, earned the bonus on the battlefields of Europe. President Hoover did not agree. "The urgent question today," he said, "is the prompt balancing of the budget. When that is accomplished, I propose to support adequate measures for relief of distress and unemployment."

Now they are camped on Anacostia Flats in the southeast corner of Washington. Nearly twenty thousand of them altogether. Everywhere you meet new ragged troups straggling in. A few have gone home discouraged, but very few. Anacostia Flats is the recruiting center; from there they are sent to new camps scattered around the outskirts of Washington. Anacostia Flats is the ghost of an army camp from the days of the big parade, with its bugle calls, its messlines, greasy K.P.'s, M.P.'s, headquarters, liaison officers, medical officer. Instead of the tents and the long tarpaper barracks of those days, the men are sleeping in little lean-tos built out of old newspapers, cardboard boxes, packing crates, bits of tin or tarpaper roofing, old shutters, every kind of cockeyed makeshift shelter from the rain scraped together out of the city dump.

The doughboys have changed too, as well as their uniforms and their housing, in these fifteen years. There's the same goulash of faces and **dialects**,[1] foreigners' pidgin English, **lingoes**[2] from industrial towns and farming towns, East, Northeast, Middle West, Southwest, South, but we were all youngsters then; now we are getting on into middle life, sunken eyes, hollow cheeks off breadlines, pale-looking knotted hands of men who've worked hard with them, and then for a long time have not worked. In these men's faces, as in Pharaoh's dream, the lean years have eaten up the fat years already. . . .

In the middle of the Anacostia camp is a big platform with a wooden object sticking up from one corner that looks like an old-fashioned gallows. Speaking goes on from this platform all morning and all afternoon. The day I saw it, there were a couple of members of the bonus army's congressional committee on the platform, a Negro in an overseas cap and a tall red Indian in buckskin and beads, wearing a ten-gallon hat. The audience, white men and Negroes, is packed in among the tents and shelters. A tall scrawny man with deeply sunken cheeks is talking. He's trying to talk about the bonus but he can't stick to it, before he knows it he's talking about the general economic conditions of the country:

---

[1] **dialects**—regional varieties of language, differing distinctively from the standard language.

[2] **lingoes**—types of jargon; strange or incomprehensible language.

"Here's a plant that can turn out everything every man, woman, and child in this country needs, from potatoes to washing machines, and it's broken down because it can't give the fellow who does the work enough money to buy what he needs with. Give us the money and we'll buy their bread and their corn and beans and their electric iceboxes and their washing machines and their radios. We ain't holding out on 'em because we don't want those things. Can't get a job to make enough money to buy 'em, that's all."

QUESTIONS TO CONSIDER

1. Who were the Bonus Army and why had they come to Washington?

2. Why can't the speaker stick to the topic of the bonus?

3. According to the platform speaker, whose fault is it that factories have had to close down?

The Bonus Army

Veterans Marched on the Capitol World War I veterans held
a peaceful march to ask for an advance on their war bonus.

20,000 Camped Out The Senate voted "No" to the early bonus payments, then voted to pay the demonstrators' way home. But many refused to leave.
▼

Hoover Used Force   Four cavalry units, four infantry companies, a machine-gun squadron, tanks, 300 policemen, and government agents moved in on the Bonus Army. The shacks the veterans had built in the shadow of the Capitol were torn down. Many people were injured.

Out of work, out of money All hope gone—men spent their days on park benches.

President Hoover's Efforts

BY JOHN GARRATY

*The Depression was not only a U. S. problem. It was a worldwide
one. In fact, President Herbert Hoover and others insisted it was
caused outside the borders of the United States. Here, historian
John Garraty writes about how Hoover viewed the causes of the
Depression and about some of the steps taken by his administration to remedy the problems.*

The Great Depression of the 1930s was a worldwide
phenomenon composed of an infinite number of separate but related events. The relationships were often
obscure; even today some of the most important of them
remain baffling. But it is indisputable that there was
a pattern to the trend of events nearly everywhere. After
the Great War of 1914–18, both **belligerents**[1] and neutrals
experienced a period of adjustment and reconstruction
that lasted until about 1925. By that date, the economies

---

[1] **belligerents**—ones who show a readiness to fight.

of most countries had gotten back at least to the levels of 1913. There followed a few years of rapid growth, but in 1929 and 1930 the prosperity ended. Then came a **precipitous**[2] plunge, which lasted until early 1933. This dark period was followed by a gradual, if spotty, recovery. The revival was **aborted**,[3] however, by the sudden, steep recession of 1937-38. Finally, a still more cataclysmic event, the outbreak of World War II in the summer of 1939, put an end to the depression.

At the time, this developing pattern was not immediately clear. The people of every country were, however, aware that the same forces were at work everywhere and that these forces had caused an economic catastrophe of unprecedented proportions.

Surely if the Great Depression was basically the same everywhere, international cooperation was essential for ending it. That much was recognized almost from the start. But despite the urgings of economists and statesmen, the nations were singularly unsuccessful in coordinating their attempts to overcome the depression. As time passed, most countries adopted narrowly nationalistic policies, some deliberately aimed at benefiting their own people at the expense of the people of other nations. Strangely, none of these divergent attacks appeared to alter the general pattern of the world economy outlined above, except that ultimately, beggar-thy-neighbor economics contributed importantly to the outbreak of World War II.

In retrospect it seems likely that if the nations had cooperated with one another better in dealing with their economic problems, they could have avoided or at least **ameliorated**[4] the terrible economic losses that all of them suffered during that decade of depression. Certainly the actions that many nations took (as well as

---

[2] **precipitous**—very steep, unusually sudden.

[3] **aborted**—terminated prematurely.

[4] **ameliorated**—improved.

some that they could have taken but did not) influenced the course of the depression in observable ways.

Knowledgeable people at the time had a good grasp of the causes of the depression, and modern experts have not added a great deal to what these observers understood. The disagreements—then and now—involve the relative importance of different factors and their interrelationships, not the causes themselves.

During the depression, politicians and businessmen and even supposedly disinterested scholars tended to blame the collapse on events that took place outside their own countries. Many still do. Since the depression was worldwide, and since what happened in one region affected conditions in many others, all such statements, whether well or ill informed, contain at least a germ of truth. But in a sense, the depression was like syphilis, which before its nature was fully understood was referred to in England as the French pox, as the Spanish disease in France, the Italian sickness in Spain, and so on. As the British civil servant Sir Arthur Salter noted in a 1932 speech about the depression, "There is a natural human tendency after any great disaster to search for a single **scapegoat**,[5] to whom the responsibility that should be shared by others may be diverted."

Many years after it ended, former President Herbert Hoover offered an elaborate explanation of the Great Depression, complete with footnote references to the work of many economists and other experts. "THE DEPRESSION WAS NOT STARTED IN THE U.S.," he insisted. The "primary cause" was the war of 1914–18. In four-fifths of the "economically sensitive" nations of the world, including such remote areas as Bolivia, Bulgaria, and Australia, the downturn was noticeable long before the 1929 collapse of American stock prices.

---

[5] **scapegoat**—someone who bears the blame for others.

Hoover blamed America's troubles on an "orgy of speculation" in the late 1920s that resulted from the cheap-money policies that the "mediocrities" who made up the majority of the Federal Reserve Board had adopted in a **futile**[6] effort to support the value of the British pound and other European currencies. Before he became president, Hoover had warned of the coming danger, but neither the board nor Hoover's predecessor, Calvin Coolidge (whom he detested), had accepted his advice. Coolidge's public statement at the end of his term that stocks were "cheap at current prices" was, Hoover believed, particularly unfortunate, since it **undermined**[7] his efforts to check the speculative mania on Wall Street after inauguration.

Hoover could not use this argument to explain the further decline that occurred in the United States in 1930, 1931, and 1932, when he was running the country. He blamed that on foreign developments. European statesmen "did not have the courage to meet the real issues," he claimed. Their rivalries and their heavy spending on arms and "frantic public works programs to meet unemployment" led to unbalanced budgets and inflation that "tore their systems asunder." The ultimate result of these unsound policies was the collapse of the German banking system in 1931; that turned what would have been no more than a minor economic downturn into the Great Depression. "The hurricane that swept our shores," wrote Hoover, "was of European origin. . . ."

The general opinion of supposedly informed people early in 1930 was that the United States had experienced no more than a minor recession, a typical stock market "panic." In June a delegation of American clergymen obtained an interview with President Hoover in order to urge him to undertake an expanded public works

---

[6] **futile**—having no result or effect; useless.

[7] **undermined**—weakened the supporting structure.

program. "You have come sixty days too late," he told them. "The depression is over."

Of course these words were scarcely out of the president's mouth when the bottom fell out of the American economy, along with the economies of most other nations. By the end of 1930, no one doubted any longer that a worldwide depression was in progress. Looking back from that vantage point, the Wall Street crash seemed the place where it had all begun.

Now, these many years later, this no longer seems correct. Scholars generally agree that American stock prices were not unreasonably high in 1929 and that the October collapse had little or no effect on the level of industrial activity in the United States or anywhere else. No effect, that is, except psychological; it is possible, though impossible to demonstrate convincingly, that the shock of the October crash so discouraged investors and consumers that a recession was turned into an economic collapse.

While all the nations experienced the same kinds of economic problems during the depression—industrial stagnation, soaring unemployment, shrinking agricultural prices, financial collapse—these problems manifested themselves in different ways in different places. What attracted the deepest concern at any given time and place appeared less pressing at others.

In the United States, Secretary of the Treasury Andrew Mellon and other conservatives, including many of the most prestigious economists, insisted that the decline should be allowed to bottom out on its own. They reasoned that the depression would eventually have a beneficial sanitizing effect on the economy. The many business bankruptcies would eliminate inefficient producers and open larger markets for efficient ones. Distress sales would get second-rate goods off the shelves and make room for better-quality products. Writing off bad debts would clear the way for fresh starts. Lowering wages would reduce costs, leading to higher profits.

People like Mellon tended to moralize about the depression. Its victims, they implied, were paying for their economic sins, getting what they deserved. Tough, hard-working, efficient types would survive; ultimately, virtue would be rewarded.

President Hoover admired Secretary Mellon, but he rejected this kind of advice. He recognized the danger that the economic slowdown might feed upon itself if nothing was done to stimulate activity. Therefore, early in the depression, he summoned business leaders to Washington and urged them to resist the temptation to cut prices, lay off some workers, and lower the wages of the rest. If manufacturers followed his advice, he predicted, profit margins and consumer demand could both be maintained.

The businessmen seemed to be impressed. Hoover also persuaded Congress to cut personal and corporation income taxes slightly to encourage spending and investment. But he did not believe that the government should intervene directly in most business matters. Doing so, he said, risked creating "a centralized despotism" that "would destroy not only our American system but with it our progress and freedom."

"Progress is born of Co-operation . . . not from governmental restraints," he said in his inaugural address. "Expansion of government in business means that the government, in order to protect itself from the political consequences of its errors, is driven irresistibly . . . to greater and greater control."

Hoover's policies failed to stop the slide. Yet when the depression deepened, he insisted that only state and local agencies and private charities could deal properly with such problems as unemployment and the relief of the **destitute.**[8] In 1930 the central section of the country

---

[8] **destitute**—one who is extremely poor, suffering great want.

was struck by a severe drought. This had nothing to do with the depression. But thousands of farmers found themselves with no harvest and not enough money to buy next year's seed or feed for their livestock. In some cases, they could not even feed their families.

Hoover quickly called a meeting of the governors of the stricken states. He proposed to create a National Drought Relief Committee, and he asked the governors to set up state committees that would in turn create county committees charged with figuring out what help was needed and how to arrange to supply it.

The elaborate structure of this drought relief plan was typical of Hoover's thinking. The federal government could provide know-how and inspiration, but the actual supervision and operation of programs should be local and in the hands of volunteers. Unfortunately, the drought relief machinery did not function properly. The local committees lacked the money needed to handle the problem. The impoverished farmers needed to borrow, but local banks were unable to supply their needs. Hoover expected the Red Cross to provide relief for the destitute, but that organization was reluctant to take on the task; it too lacked sufficient resources and hesitated to commit the limited funds it did have to drought relief.

Hoover's plan did not work. Yet he continued to insist that "mutual self-help through voluntary giving" was the proper way to deal with such situations. Furthermore, when shrinking federal revenues resulting from the depression caused the government to run at a deficit, Hoover forgot about trying to stimulate consumer spending. He called for tax increases and reduced government outlays in order to balance the budget. In 1932, as the depression sounded the depths, Congress *raised* taxes by a larger percentage than ever before in American history.

By the end of 1930, the American banking system was in serious trouble. Over 1,300 banks had failed during the year, and the number was increasing rapidly. The harm caused by these failures—both the actual loss of savings and the fear that the failures inspired among depositors with money in other, "sound" banks was so great that Hoover recognized that something had to be done.

But he did not ask Congress for legislation or order the secretary of the treasury to do anything. Instead he called a secret meeting of the country's leading bankers. They were caught in "a degenerating vicious cycle," he told them. It was essential "to restore confidence in the people at large." At his urging, the bankers reluctantly agreed to form a National Credit Corporation (despite its name, this was not a government body) and provide it with $500 million to lend to shaky banks.

President Hoover took pride in having dealt with the problem in the "American way." But the solution he devised provided too little relief and it came too late. The bankers who ran the National Credit Corporation hesitated to lend their precious $500 million to the banks that needed it most. They became, in Hoover's own words, "ultraconservative, then fearful" and the corporation finally died. During 1931, while Hoover continued to stress maintaining the sound fiscal position of the federal government, nearly 2,300 more banks failed.

In 1932, with Hoover's somewhat reluctant approval, Congress created the Reconstruction Finance Corporation (RFC). This was a federal agency empowered to lend money to troubled banks, insurance companies, railroads, and state and local governments. The RFC was modeled on the War Finance Corporation, which had lent money for plant expansion to companies engaged in war production in 1917–18. Another measure, the Glass-Steagall Act, authorized the Federal Reserve Banks to make loans on assets not previously permissible under the law. These measures prevented many business bankruptcies and kept hundreds of banks from having to close their doors. But in early 1933, just before Franklin Roosevelt took office, the banking system collapsed, precipitating a crisis that led to more basic financial reforms.

QUESTIONS TO CONSIDER

1. Why did many scholars and politicians blame the Depression on forces outside their own countries?

2. What steps did Hoover take to end the Depression?

3. In your opinion, what are the lessons for our current government that can be taken from the experience of the Depression?

The Biggest Thing Except for Wars

BY J. DOUGLAS BROWN

Hoover had many programs that were aimed at encouraging the business community to provide solutions to the widespread unemployment. None of these programs really worked. The author was teaching economics at Princeton University when he was invited to join the Hoover administration in fighting the Depression. He shares his first-hand impressions of the problem and of President Hoover.

The Hoover administration was getting terribly concerned in '30: The economic effects of the Crash were growing very rapidly, and Hoover was in over his head. He picked a man named Colonel Wood, who had formerly been police commissioner of the city of New York and was well-to-do in his own right, to form a committee on the economic crisis. Wood searched around immediately for people who knew something, and I was picked from Princeton.

So I went down to Washington and worked 14 hours a day. My area was to help get the employer to take care of unemployment himself, by having employees share work. The idea was that the employer, instead of holding one person full time and laying off another, would cut both people's hours in half, so that each would work two and a half days a week. We developed a nationwide radio campaign, in which we got the presidents of the great corporations on national radio for 15 minutes at prime time to make these **appeals.**[1]

Then I developed a four-page outline of the steps needed to spread the work. The printing office printed about three million and sent them all over the country. Then we did another outline, which was called "Easy Steps." We also put advertisements in subways and all sorts of other places all over the country, and got good cooperation with our campaign slogan: "Spread the Work!"

Meanwhile, we did lots of other things, and one of them was the reason we got fired. We were trying to impress upon Hoover that he had to set up an administration immediately to get after unemployment. He had argued that the Red Cross was set up for this; but it was utterly impossible to think of the Red Cross in that context. We said that we must get public works started, and asked for $450 million. Hoover just thought we were **radicals.**[2] He was willing to go up to only $150 million for public works for the whole country. Just think of it. It was a drop in the bucket compared with what we thought was needed. And he finally thought we had gone too far and let us go.

Hoover was in his hair-shirt[3] period then. He had a man who reported to him up on the Hill, and as far as

---

[1] **appeals**—earnest requests or pleas.

[2] **radicals**—political groups associated with views, practices, and policies of extreme change.

[3] hair shirt—a shirt made of rough animal hair and worn next to the skin as a punishment.

we could tell, that man would never tell Congress what we were recommending; he'd play it down. Take that $450 million. I don't think Hoover ever let that go to Congress. And since we were his advisors, we couldn't go out and announce some of these things.

He was a man in a hell of a hole, and it seemed as though he couldn't fully understand why. I remember, my wife and I went to a presidential reception, and after we went through the reception line to meet Hoover, my wife said, "I looked right in his face and it was perfectly gray. I mean, his whole **demeanor**[4] was just that of a very tired, discouraged man." And I think that was true.

Sure the government and the American people were scared. This was the biggest thing that had hit them except for wars—and in wartime at least you knew what to do. You knew you had to get out production; you knew you had to train troops. But in the case of the depression, the American people were frustrated, because the vast majority didn't know what to do. They felt that it was up to the government, and the government wasn't operating. Those were desperate times—which is why Roosevelt got in by such a terrific landslide.

---

[4] **demeanor**—outward manner or behavior.

QUESTIONS TO CONSIDER

1. Why was Brown so committed to selling employers on the idea of job-sharing?

2. Do you think Hoover's firing of Brown was justified? Why or why not?

3. What do you think about the way Hoover handled the Depression? Do you feel any sympathy for Hoover, the "man in a hell of a hole"?

Red Cross Relief . . . for Who?

BY WILL ROGERS

The humorist, actor, and writer Will Rogers (1879–1935) was born on Oologah, Indian Territory (now Oklahoma). His full name was William Penn Adair Rogers. He commented on life around him in books with names like The Cowboy Philosopher on Prohibition *and* Illiterate Digest. *In syndicated newspaper articles he displayed a dry, biting humor and homespun philosophy that enjoyed a very wide audience. Here's an example of one of his zingers.*

You talk about this country being hard up, every place thinks it's worse off than the other. The Red Cross, as usual, is doing heroic work, but it's the people that they can't reach, people that they never heard of, people that are so far back in the woods that the rest of the world has almost forgotten 'em. Those are the ones that I pity in all this depression. I am speaking of the Senate and Congress of these United States.

I want to see a Red Cross relief formed that will go so far back into the underbrush of the **hinterland**[1] that it will reach this little known but patriotic group.

Then can the Red Cross say, "We have performed our duty."

---

[1] **hinterland**—a region remote from urban areas or cultural centers.

QUESTIONS TO CONSIDER

1. What is Rogers' attitude toward the Senate and Congress?

2. In your opinion, is his assessment of government fair?

3. Why does Rogers emphasize the government's patriotism?

FDR and the
New Deal

"The Only Thing We Have to Fear Is Fear Itself"

BY FRANKLIN DELANO ROOSEVELT

Franklin Delano Roosevelt was elected overwhelmingly in the presidential election of November, 1932. By the time of his inauguration on March 4, 1933, the nation was locked in a terrible banking crisis. The governors of New York and Illinois declared banking holidays, which shut down the great financial centers in New York City and Chicago. All the security and commodity exchanges except the Chicago Livestock Exchange also closed. The speech Roosevelt gave that day, following his taking the oath of office, is one of the great speeches in American history. His words were met with huge waves of applause. All over the country, people listened to his speech on the radio. He asked for support from the people. He also said he would ask Congress for broad powers, like those given to a president in wartime, to fight the current emergency.

President Hoover, Mr. Chief Justice, my friends:

This is a day of national **consecration,**[1] and I am certain that my fellow-Americans expect that on my induction into the Presidency I will address them with a **candor**[2] and a decision which the present situation of our nation impels.

This is pre-eminently the time to speak the truth, the whole truth, frankly and boldly. Nor need we shrink from honestly facing conditions in our country today. This great nation will endure as it has endured, will revive and will prosper.

So first of all let me assert my firm belief that the only thing we have to fear is fear itself—nameless, unreasoning, unjustified terror which paralyzes needed efforts to convert retreat into advance.

In every dark hour of our national life a leadership of frankness and vigor has met with that understanding and support of the people themselves which is essential to victory. I am convinced that you will again give that support to leadership in these critical days.

In such a spirit on my part and on yours we face our common difficulties. They concern, thank God, only material things. Values have shrunken to fantastic levels; taxes have risen; our ability to pay has fallen, government of all kinds is faced by serious curtailment of income; the means of exchange are frozen in the currents of trade; the withered leaves of industrial enterprise lie on every side; farmers find no markets for their produce; the savings of many years in thousands of families are gone.

More important, a host of unemployed citizens face the grim problem of existence, and an equally great

---

[1] **consecration**—the induction into an office; devotion to a purpose with deep dedication.

[2] **candor**—unreserved, honest, sincere expressions.

number toil with little return. Only a foolish optimist can deny the dark realities of the moment.

Yet our distress comes from no failure of substance. We are stricken by no plague of locusts. Compared with the perils which our forefathers conquered because they believed and were not afraid, we have still much to be thankful for. Nature still offers her bounty and human efforts have multiplied it. Plenty is at our doorstep, but a generous use of it **languishes**[3] in the very sight of the supply.

Primarily, this is because the rulers of the exchange of mankind's goods have failed through their own stubbornness and their own incompetence, have admitted that failure and **abdicated**.[4] Practices of the **unscrupulous**[5] money changers stand indicted in the court of public opinion, rejected by the hearts and minds of men.

True, they have tried, but their efforts have been cast in the pattern of an outworn tradition. Faced by failure of credit, they have proposed only the lending of more money.

Stripped of the lure of profit by which to induce our people to follow their false leadership, they have resorted to **exhortations**,[6] pleading tearfully for restored confidence. They know only the rules of a generation of self-seekers.

They have no vision, and when there is no vision the people perish.

The money changers have fled from their high seats in the temple of our civilization. We may now restore that temple to the ancient truths.

---

[3] **languishes**—loses strength or force.

[4] **abidicated**—gave up power, responsibility, or an office.

[5] **unscrupulous**—without scruples; unprincipled; contemptuous of what is right.

[6] **exhortations**—speeches intended to advise, incite, or encourage.

The measure of the restoration lies in the extent to which we apply social values more noble than mere monetary profit.

Happiness lies not in the mere possession of money; it lies in the joy of achievement, in the thrill of creative effort.

The joy and moral stimulation of work no longer must be forgotten in the mad chase of **evanescent**[7] profits. These dark days will be worth all they cost us if they teach us that our true destiny is not to be ministered unto but to minister to ourselves and to our fellow-men.

Recognition of the falsity of material wealth as the standard of success goes hand in hand with the abandonment of the false belief that public office and high political position are to be valued only by the standards of pride of place and personal profit; and there must be an end to a conduct in banking and in business which too often has given to a sacred trust the likeness of callous and selfish wrongdoing.

Small wonder that confidence languishes, for it thrives only on honesty, on honor, on the sacredness of obligations, on faithful protection, on unselfish performance. Without them it cannot live.

Restoration calls, however, not for changes in ethics alone. This nation asks for action, and action now.

Our greatest primary task is to put people to work. This is no unsolvable problem if we face it wisely and courageously . . .

I favor as a practical policy the putting of first things first. I shall spare no effort to restore world trade by international economic readjustment, but the emergency at home cannot wait on that accomplishment.

The basic thought that guides these specific means of national recovery is not narrowly nationalistic.

---

[7] **evanescent**—not lasting; tending to vanish like vapor.

It is the insistence, as a first consideration, upon the interdependence of the various elements in, and parts of, the United States—a recognition of the old and permanently important manifestation of the American spirit of the pioneer.

It is the way to recovery. It is the immediate way. It is the strongest assurance that the recovery will endure.

In the field of world policy I would dedicate this nation to the policy of the good neighbor—the neighbor who resolutely respects himself and, because he does so, respects the rights of others—the neighbor who respects his obligations and respects the sanctity of his agreements in and with a world of neighbors.

If I read the temper of our people correctly, we now realize as we have never before, our interdependence on each other; that we cannot merely take, but we must give as well; that if we are to go forward we must move as a trained and loyal army willing to sacrifice for the good of a common discipline, because, without such discipline, no progress is made, no leadership becomes effective.

We are, I know, ready and willing to submit our lives and property to such discipline because it makes possible a leadership which aims at a larger good.

This I propose to offer, pledging that the larger purposes will bind upon us all as a sacred obligation with a unity of duty hitherto evoked only in time of armed strife.

With this pledge taken, I assume unhesitatingly the leadership of this great army of our people, dedicated to a disciplined attack upon our common problems.

Action in this image and to this end is feasible under the forms of government which we have inherited from our ancestors.

Our Constitution is so simple and practical that it is possible always to meet extraordinary needs by changes in emphasis and arrangement without loss of essential form.

That is why our constitutional system has proved itself the most superbly enduring political mechanism the modern world has produced. It has met every stress of vast expansion of territory, of foreign wars, of bitter internal strife, of world relations . . .

I am prepared under my constitutional duty to recommend the measures that a stricken nation in the midst of a stricken world may require.

These measures, or such other measures as the Congress may build out of its experience and wisdom, I shall seek, within my constitutional authority, to bring to speedy adoption.

But in the event that the Congress shall fail to take one of these two courses, and in the event that the national emergency is still critical, I shall not evade the clear course of duty that will then confront me.

I shall ask the Congress for the one remaining instrument to meet the crisis—broad executive power to wage a war against the emergency as great as the power that would be given me if we were in fact invaded by a foreign foe.

For the trust reposed in me I will return the courage and the devotion that befit the time. I can do no less.

We face the **arduous**[8] days that lie before us in the warm courage of national unity; with the clear consciousness of seeking old and precious moral values; with the clean satisfaction that comes from the stern performance of duty by old and young alike.

We aim at the assurance of a rounded and permanent national life.

We do not distrust the future of essential democracy. The people of the United States have not failed. In their need they have registered a mandate that they want direct, vigorous action.

---

[8] **arduous**—extremely difficult, laborious, strenuous.

They have asked for discipline and direction under leadership. They have made me the present instrument of their wishes. In the spirit of the gift I take it.

In this dedication of a nation we humbly ask the blessing of God. May He protect each and every one of us! May He guide me in the days to come!

QUESTIONS TO CONSIDER

1. To what fears was Roosevelt probably referring when he said that the only thing we have to fear is fear itself?

2. In what ways does Roosevelt imply that the country will be better off under his leadership than that of the previous administration?

3. Why doesn't Roosevelt consider monetary profit to be the primary measure of a recovery?

4. In your opinion, should a president have broad executive power to wage war against emergencies? Explain why or why not.

The First One Hundred Days

BY CABELL PHILLIPS

Immediately upon being elected, Roosevelt changed the style of presidency. He began his "fireside chats," the regular radio addresses he made to the American people. And he asked for, and got, immediate approval from Congress for a wide range of programs. Humorists labeled these programs "alphabet soup" because they became known by their initials, such as CCC, WPA, and TVA. This selection describes what occurred during the first hundred days of his administration.

The Roosevelt Administration's fabled "Hundred Days"—probably as crucial a brief epoch as any in the nation's history—had started. They were to **dissipate**[1] the panic of the Depression even if they would not break the back of the Depression itself. In virtually his first official act in office, initiated within hours of taking the oath, the President decreed a national bank holiday,

---

[1] **dissipate**—to break up and drive off.

shutting down every financial institution in the land, and called a special session of Congress to convene within four days. Simultaneously, a dozen task forces were at work drafting one of the most revolutionary legislative programs ever essayed by any President. Between March 9 and June 16 Roosevelt would propose and Congress would pass fifteen "emergency" acts, which, in their totality, would drastically affect the nation's social and political orientation far into the future. Some of these laws were temporary stop-gaps and some would in time be struck down by the courts, but fully half of these "emergency" enactments remain embedded in the statute books today. Never before had such a legislative miracle been wrought in so short a time.

"Whatever laws the President thinks he may need to end the depression," Senator Burton K. Wheeler of Montana said on Inauguration Day, "Congress will jump through a hoop to put them through." His prophecy was fulfilled.

Many urged the President to request—or to seize— the powers of a dictator. "The President's program demands dictatorial authority," the Boston *Transcript* editorialized toward the end of the first week. "This is unprecedented in its implications, but such is the desperate temper of the people that it is welcome."

All across the country there was a sudden upsurge of support and enthusiasm for the new President. At last, people told one another, *something* was being done: the perilous drift toward ruin and revolution was being checked. Even the closing of the banks, as bad as it was for many, was a welcome break in the suspense of not knowing what would happen next. It appeared that whatever the new President decided to do, the people were ready to go along with him. They **deluged**[2] him

---

[2] **deluged**—flooded, inundated.

with messages of **fealty**[3] and good wishes. Some 14,000 letters and telegrams poured into the White House mailroom during the first week alone. The New York *Daily News,* which had not backed Roosevelt in the election, grudgingly conceded it might have been wrong and said, "This newspaper pledges itself to support the policies of FDR for a period of at least one year; longer if circumstances warrant." And Alfred M. Landon of Kansas, who was to loom large in the life of Roosevelt four years later, affirmed: "If there is any way in which a Republican governor of a midwestern state can aid the President in the fight, I now enlist for the duration of the war."

FDR was quickly revealed as a man of action, and as a man of warmth and feeling as well. Hoover, a **mirthless**[4] man under the best of circumstances, had, under the most trying of circumstances, cast a **pall**[5] of cheerless **austerity**[6] over the White House. This evaporated instantly as the big, **garrulous**[7] family of Roosevelts, with their gaiety and informality, moved in. The mood projected itself to official Washington and to the world beyond. The President attacked his job with zest and enthusiasm. At his first press conference he stunned the hundred-odd reporters who crowded into his office by his friendly, relaxed manner, the first-name intimacy with which he addressed many of them, and the candor and liberality with which he answered their questions. "The most amazing performance of its kind in the White House ever seen," is the way a correspondent for the Baltimore *Sun* described this encounter.

President Hoover had dourly told Roosevelt that "a President calls on no one." But FDR found an hour

---

[3] **fealty**—loyalty, allegiance.

[4] **mirthless**—humorless.

[5] **pall**—something that covers, darkens, or produces a gloomy effect.

[6] **austerity**—gravity, somberness.

[7] **garrulous**—very talkative.

during that crowded week to call at the home of retired Justice Oliver Wendell Holmes on the occasion of the great jurist's ninety-second birthday.

On the evening of Sunday, March 12, as the finale of his first week in office, Roosevelt opened a line of communication directly to the people themselves. It was an intimate way of talking to a vast radio audience—the fireside chat, which he made uniquely his own. These radio "visits" by the President of the United States into the American living room were a triumph of the dramatic art that no other public figure has ever matched. So deftly were they done, so subtle were their histrionics and so free of pretensions or obvious guile, that one could feel the presence of Roosevelt as one listened to his words. In this first fireside chat he spoke as a wise friend speaks to his neighbors, telling them in simple, believable words why their banks were closed and what was being done to get them open again. He did not patronize his listeners with platitudes and false promises. The banking system was truly in a bad way, he said, and some people were going to be hurt before the damage could be repaired. But there would be far fewer victims now than if the crisis were allowed to run its course, and when the banks would reopen in a few days they would be stronger than before.

It was a masterful performance. It helped to restore the people's confidence and built a bridge of intimacy between them and the President. . . .

Imagine what it would be like *today* to wake up one morning to discover that the government had shut every bank in the nation; that all the money you could lay your hands on was what you had in your pocket, and that you couldn't get any more when that was spent. Would hysterical mobs go screaming through the streets, storming the banks with crowbars and dynamite, looting the stores for food and weapons? Would the well-to-do rush to bury their jewels and family plate under the cellar floor, and farmers sit with shotguns across their laps to repel invasion by hungry city mobs?

Well, nothing of the sort happened on that historic Monday more than three decades ago. Some individuals probably did panic; some rushed in disbelief to their banks to find out if the news was really true; some housewives took all the change they could scrape together and converted it into a hoard of salt meat and canned goods at the grocery store. But they were the exception. Among the people as a whole the reaction was just the opposite. The shutting of banks snapped the bonds of tension and uncertainty that had bound them for weeks. Suddenly the agony of fear and waiting was over. Something that everybody could understand had happened, something as clear and unequivocal as a clap of thunder at midnight. There was a sense of relief, the kind of euphoria that comes with a sudden release from pain. Grim, even tragic, though the provocation was, people could laugh and make jokes about their common dilemma—at the outset at least.

The experiences that people endured in a moneyless society were immensely varied, some of them painful and comic. Salesmen stranded in cities away from their homes hawked the contents of their sample cases in hotel lobbies—shoes, jewelry, patent medicines, wearing apparel—to get money for train fare. Businessmen met their payrolls with postdated checks, promissory notes, company-backed scrip, merchandise from their inventories. Hotels and restaurants went on an all-credit basis; so did grocers, dairies, drugstores and gasoline stations for their regular customers. Soon the most critical shortage became not money per se but currency in usable denominations and in coins. With only a twenty-dollar bill in your wallet you were as bad as broke if you wanted to buy cigarettes or ride in a taxi. Shopkeepers cruised the streets looking for newsboys and apple vendors who would sell them 80 cents worth of change for a dollar bill. New York commuters drained the ready cash reserves of the Long Island Railroad by cashing in their commutation tickets. Patronage at movie houses fell almost to zero. The promoters of a boxing tournament at Madison Square Garden accepted any kind of usable barter for tickets, including, it was said, a pair of ladies' silk panties. In Miami the American Express Company put a $50 limit on the amount of a vacationer's checks it would redeem, and a hotel in the Chicago Loop discovered that under its benevolent "stay-now, pay-later" plan it was playing host to a number of **denizens**[8] of the nearby skid row.[9]

For many millions the novelty and the humor of the situation was a pretty thin veneer that quickly wore through. Few wage earners could afford to miss a single payday without encountering distress. Few had even a blocked bank account on which they could draw checks, nor did they have credit beyond the needs of a day or two at the corner grocer. Raising carfare to get to and from work or school or a source of charity was a family problem. Relief applications soared. Thousands began to suffer from hunger and cold. In Detroit, where the bank holiday was in its fourth week, business activity was off 60 percent. Some municipal workers, with uncashable pay checks in their pockets, fainted on the job for lack of food.

Scrip[10] showed up in different forms in scores of cities. It was issued to employees in lieu of real wages by municipalities and by private concerns. The city of Cleveland circulated thousands of scrip "dollar bills" signed by the mayor and treasurer. A three-cent stamp had to be affixed each time a scrip changed hands. When a bill had acquired thirty-six stamps, the city promised to redeem it for $1.08 in "real" money. A resort

---

[8] **denizens**—inhabitants.

[9] skid row—an area where the poor, homeless, and unemployed live.

[10] scrip—a token or piece of paper used in place of money in emergencies.

hotel in Pasadena printed its own scrip, which the railroads accepted to get the hotel's guests back to their homes. The *Daily Princetonian* printed scrip in 25-cent denominations for the use of its student subscribers. Telephone slugs, postage stamps, bus and subway tokens, foreign coins, and even cigarette coupons all played a vital role in this "funny money" epic of the great bank holiday.

When Congress convened in special session at noon on Thursday, March 9, Secretary of the Treasury Woodin had ready for it the draft of an emergency banking bill. It had been written and rewritten, cut and trimmed and pasted together through many hours of arduous labor during the preceding four days. What it did, in effect, was to validate the President's bank-closing proclamation of Monday, including the penalties for hoarding or using gold. It gave the Treasury power to grant or withhold licenses for the reopening of banks and to appoint "conservators" for the shakier ones, and it authorized the issuance of Federal Reserve notes if necessary to replenish the currency supply.

There was not time enough to have the bill printed. The half-dozen typewritten copies that were rushed to the Capitol the morning of March 9 still bore marginal notes and corrections scribbled in pencil. In the House of Representatives there was no pretense of committee consideration. Only a few of the leaders had even seen the text. As the House reading clerk finished reading the one copy available in that chamber, cries went up from the floor, "Vote, vote!" Thirty-eight minutes later the bill was passed by acclamation. The Senate was slightly more deliberate. It listened to three hours of debate, most of it stimulated by Huey Long's clamorous pleas in behalf of "the little state banks at the forks of the creek," before passing the bill 73 to 7. At 8:37 that night, FDR, with newsreel cameras focused on his desk in the

White House, signed the first legislative enactment of the New Deal.

The psychological impact of this swift, bold stroke was enormous. Its first manifestation occurred the next day, Friday. Gold hoarders by the thousands queued up before the regional Reserve banks in New York and elsewhere to get rid of the yellow treasure, which had suddenly become **contraband.**[11] It was "a gold rush in reverse," said *The New York Times,* "unlike anything in the memory of the downtown banking community." Expensively dressed men and women, some of them carrying packages and valises filled with gold coins and certificates, stood patiently in line to convert their hoards to legal tender. An armored truck drove up with the $6 million in bullion[12] said to have been the nest egg of an unnamed but obviously jittery corporation. Housewives and teenagers and grandparents joined the line to push personal coin collections through the tellers' wickets. (Small, sentimental holdings such as these were later omitted from the ban.) By Saturday night the Federal Reserve System had recovered $300 million in gold—enough to back up the issuance of $750 million in new currency.

Under the emergency legislation, controlled reopening of the banks was to be permitted beginning on Monday, March 13. Treasury officials had divided the nation's banks—about 5,000 national banks, members of the Federal Reserve System, and about 14,000 non-member state banks—into three categories of relative solvency. Class A banks, numbering about 2,400, were adjudged to be in sufficiently good shape to reopen at once. Class B banks would need some sort of shoring up before they would be permitted to reopen. Class C banks numbering about 900, would have to remain

---

[11] **contraband**—forbidden goods.

[12] bullion—gold or silver.

closed for the time being at least, under a "conservator," appointed by the Treasury.

The men at the Treasury worked furiously that week at the formidable task of grading and licensing some 19,000 individual banks. (The strain broke Woodin's frail health; he resigned in November and died within a year.) One of the most feared imponderables was whether, when the banks did open their doors again, still panicky depositors would withdraw their money and start the lethal bleeding process all over again. Roosevelt's fireside chat on Sunday night was designed to avert just such a reaction, though there was no assurance that the remedy would work.

But by noon on that critical Monday it was clear that the panic was over. All but nine of New York City's 140 banks reopened for "business as usual" at 9 A.M., and there were openings in similar proportions in other cities up and down the eastern seaboard and westward. There were uncommonly long lines at the tellers' windows, but the majority of customers were putting more money into their accounts (putting it *back,* possibly) than they were taking out. In New York City alone, deposits exceeded withdrawals that day by $10 million, and this pattern was repeated in major banking centers all across the country. At the end of the week approximately 75 percent of the Nation's banks were back in business. The New York Stock Exchange and the Chicago commodity markets—unleashed along with the banks— had one of their best weeks since September 1932. And an $800 million refinancing offering by the Treasury, which most officials had anticipated with dread, was oversubscribed two and a half times.

One day at midweek hundreds of stock tickers in brokers' offices around the country carried this greeting from an exuberant Wall Street teletype operator: "Happy Days Are Here Again." Most people agreed. . . .

The legislative leaders had come to the White House on Wednesday night to be briefed on the emergency banking bill, which they would receive on the following day. When this part of the discussion was over, the President went on in a disarmingly casual, conversational way, to say that he would have "a pretty important" economy bill for them on Friday. Most of them would agree, he observed airily, that Hoover's extravagance had led the country close to bankruptcy. And he reminded them that the Democratic platform called for a 25 percent cut in federal spending and a balanced budget. Well, he was ready to show the country he meant business on economy, just as he had on the banking crisis. The new bill would call for slashing veterans' benefits almost in half—by $400 million—and for cutting government salaries, including those of members of the Congress, by another $100 million.

The legislators were aghast. The veterans' lobby was one of the most powerful in the nation and had successfully resisted every previous attempt to curtail their pensions and other prerequisites. They were too potent politically, the legislators protested, to be offended in this way at the very outset of the new Administration. And as for the salary cuts, they went on, quite aside from the financial burden it would bring to individual members of Congress, there was a sizable bloc in both houses who felt that such a deflationary[13] measure was just the opposite of what the economy needed.

Roosevelt was unimpressed. He had no strong views of his own on this complex economic issue, but he admired Lew Douglas, to whom this sort of fiscal **orthodoxy**[14] was the keystone of recovery. He was anxious, too, to reassure the business community that

---

[13] deflationary—a decrease in the amount of available money that results in a drop in prices.

[14] **orthodoxy**—strict adherence to the traditional belief.

his would be a "sound" Administration, one that they need not fear. This was perhaps the most profound contradiction of the early New Deal. Very shortly FDR would switch to deficit financing on a huge scale as blithely as he now embraced pay-as-you-go.

The economy bill reached Capitol Hill on Friday, while Congress was still spinning from its encounters with the banking bill. As the leaders had prophesied, it caused sparks to fly. Representative Joseph W. Byrns, the new Democratic floor leader, refused to sponsor it in the House. Speaker Henry T. Rainey tried but failed to get a binding vote of support from the Democratic caucus. However, a handful of loyalists rallied the troops, arguing that the President would know by their votes "whether the members of his own party were willing to go along with him in his fight to save the country." Though the bill passed 266 to 138, it was a closer shave than the score indicated. Ninety-two Democrats deserted their leader, but sixty-nine Republicans swung over to sustain him. Without those Republican votes the Hundred Days might have been fatally foreshortened then and there.

Even more trouble was expected in the Senate, which planned to take up the economy bill on Monday. Discussing the outlook with a small group of friends at dinner Sunday evening, FDR was seized with a sudden inspiration. "You know," he said, tilting his cigarette holder skyward, "this would be a good time for beer." He sent for a copy of the Democratic platform, snipped out the plank on Prohibition, and wrote a seventy-two-word message calling for the immediate legalization of light beer and wine.

The message, totally unexpected, went to Congress on Monday. Its effect was like that of the carrot on the stick to get a balky donkey in motion, just as Roosevelt had intended it to be. That day the economy bill won a

60 to 20 test vote in the Senate. On Tuesday the House passed the beer bill 316 to 97. On Wednesday the Senate cleared the economy bill 62 to 13, and the next day it passed the beer bill. . . .

After the banking and economy acts, other major programs came into existence in quick succession during the Hundred Days. . . . It is an incredible catalogue of bills submitted to, and enacted by, the Congress. In each case, the introductory date in the listing is the date of submission to Congress:

March 16—Agricultural Adjustment Act (enacted May 12). The draft presented to Congress was a composite of several plans, old and new, for raising farm income and reducing surpluses. Essentially, it offered subsidies to farmers who agreed to restrict their planting of certain basic crops. Subsidies were to be derived from a processing tax paid by manufacturers (e.g., flour millers), a provision that later proved to be the legal undoing of this statute. The bill included an important amendment giving the President wide authority to bring about inflation by reducing the gold content of the dollar and by issuing greenbacks.

March 21—Civilian Conservation Corps (enacted March 31). The CCC was an original idea of FDR's, stimulated by his longtime interests in forestry and conservation. He proposed to take 250,000 unemployed young men off the streets and welfare rolls and give them jobs at $30 a month plus keep for doing useful work in forests and national parks. This work program for youths was the first and most widely approved of a variety of work relief programs that were to follow. Within a week after enactment the first CCC camp opened near Luray, Virginia, with an enrollment of 2,500.

March 21—Federal Emergency Relief Act (enacted May 12). Roosevelt asked for an appropriation of $500 million for a direct assault on unemployment and drought through loans and grants to the states. The act creating the Federal Emergency Relief Administration was soon followed by further laws providing jobs for the unemployed on public works: the short-lived Civil Works Administration (CWA), the Works Progress Administration (WPA), and the longer-ranged, slower-paced Public Works Administration (PWA). Harry Hopkins, whose name would become as nearly synonymous with the New Deal as Roosevelt's, was named FERA Administrator. (PWA shortly came under the jurisdiction of Harold Ickes.)

March 27—Farm Credit Administration. By Executive Order, the President established the FCA, a single agency combining activities of half a dozen agencies dealing with farm credit: the Federal Farm Board, Federal Land Banks, the Agricultural Credit Corporation, etc. The purpose was to centralize in one place all farm credit services. Legislation was enacted June 16 to complete the merger. Henry Morgenthau, Jr., was appointed FCA Governor. (Later he succeeded William H. Woodin as Secretary of the Treasury.)

March 29—"Truth in Securities" Act (enacted May 27). In submitting this bill to Congress, FDR said: "This proposal adds to the ancient rule of *caveat emptor* the further doctrine, 'Let the seller also beware.'" The bill required the seller of securities to disclose fully all pertinent information about them; empowered the Federal Trade Commission to block the sale of misrepresented securities; and imposed stiff penalties for violators. The name "Truth in Securities" of this act is a synonym for the Securities Act of 1933, which was only half the legislative package dealing with securities; the regulatory half was provided in the Securities Exchange Act of 1934.

April 10—Tennessee Valley Authority Act (enacted May 18). In one bold stroke FDR resolved a controversy that had raged between liberals and conservatives for a decade. He asserted the government's right to own and operate for the public good the huge hydroelectric and manufacturing facility at Muscle Shoals, Alabama, built during the World War at a cost of more than $165 million. It had stood idle while the advocates of public and private power battled for its possession. FDR not only came down on the side of public ownership but vastly enlarged the scope of the undertaking to make it the world's outstanding example of regional conservation and economic development.

April 13—Home Owners Loan Act (enacted June 13). The provisions of this act did for the urban homeowner what the Farm Mortgage Act did for the farmer: it averted foreclosures and the eviction of tens of thousands of families unable to keep up existing mortgage payments. With a revolving fund of $2 billion raised through the issuance of bonds, the Home Owners' Loan Corporation refinanced individual home mortgages up to $14,000 at 5 percent interest for a maximum of fifteen years.

April 19—Abandonment of the Gold Standard (by Executive Order). The pressure for inflation—to get more money in circulation—had become so intense by mid-April, particularly from Congress, that Roosevelt was faced with the choice of either submitting to it or managing it. He chose the latter. His Executive Order *permanently* embargoed all exports of gold (a temporary embargo had been ordered on March 6), which left the dollar free to find its level among the other devalued currencies of the world.

May 4—Railroad Coordination Act (enacted June 16). The nation's railroads, most of them afloat on Reconstruction Finance Corporation loans, were in as depressed a condition as any segment of industry. The bill submitted on May 4 represented an effort, tentative at best, to enforce economies by consolidation and rate-making reforms, with the ultimate view (never realized) of creating a coordinated transportation system. Joseph B. Eastman was moved from the Interstate Commerce Commission to be Federal Coordinator of Transportation.

May 17—National Industrial Recovery Act (enacted June 16). The NIRA was the crowning legislative achievement of the Hundred Days and one of the most conspicuous, if least durable, monuments of the entire New Deal. A patchwork of many schemes and ideas, it vested in the President unprecedented peacetime powers to manage the business life of the nation down to the smallest unit. The National Recovery Administration (NRA), established under the NIRA, gave the nation business "codes" with the force of law, the thirty-hour week, minimum-wage rates, the symbolic Blue Eagle, Gen. Hugh "Iron Pants" Johnson, and almost three years of unremitting turmoil, excitement, hope, and despair.

May 17—Glass-Steagall Banking Act (enacted June 16). This law was not, strictly speaking, a New Deal measure, for it had been gestating in Congressional committees for two years. But it fitted the New Deal pattern of reform, and the New Deal provided the impetus for its ultimate passage. It forced commercial banks to get out of the investment business, and it established, over the loud protest of most orthodox bankers, insurance of deposits in national banks under the Federal Deposit Insurance Corporation.

May 26—Annulment of Gold Clause in Contracts (enacted June 5). Most government obligations (bonds, currency, etc.) and many private contracts called for payment in gold—that is, dollars with a specific gold content (23.22 grains). The continued existence of this requirement virtually nullified the President's recently won powers to inflate the currency. Enactment of the measure meant the final breakaway from the gold standard.

QUESTIONS TO CONSIDER

1. Why do you think that President Roosevelt chose to legalize beer and wine at the same time that he proposed his economy bill?

2. How did President Roosevelt's fireside chat help him win public confidence?

3. Why was the emergency banking bill an important first step in reducing the panic of the Depression?

4. What made Roosevelt's economy bill more controversial than his banking bill?

5. Why were Roosevelt's first hundred days in office significant?

Clifford Kennedy Berryman's Cartoons Newspapers across the country carried Berryman's cartoons. He shows a confident Roosevelt, but he reflects the views of Roosevelt's critics.

An American who had left the country 21 years earlier because of too much government in business is shown returning to find Uncle Sam surrounded by the alphabet letters of New Deal programs.

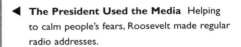

◀ The President Used the Media Helping to calm people's fears, Roosevelt made regular radio addresses.

Families Listened Together Before television, familes gathered around the radio. Here a Kansas farm family hears Roosevelt.

▼

WPA, CCC, PWA and CWA These government programs were created to employ the unemployed. Some were very shortlived, while others, like the WPA, became synonymous with the New Deal. ▶

This is a Civilian Conservation Corps (CCC) jazz band. The CCC employed young men aged 18–25 in a variety of projects that helped the nation. ▼

◀ CCC at work building a retaining wall at George Washington National Forest, Virginia.

George Biddle at work on a WPA mural.

▲
Smithfield, N.C. A Farm Security Administration supervisor discusses the cotton crop with one of the clients.

A U.S. Resettlement Administration client repays his loan. ▶

Getting By

from

The Dust Bowl

JANELLE YATES' BIOGRAPHY
OF WOODY GUTHRIE

As if things weren't bad enough in the 1930s, the world was plagued by a series of severe droughts. In the grasslands states of Kansas, Oklahoma, Texas, New Mexico, and Colorado, where farming and cattle-raising had deprived the land of the grasses that held it together, great quantities of topsoil was blown away. Winds blew the dust up into enormous dark clouds. In some cases it blew as far away as the Atlantic Ocean. Edward Robb Ellis said that in a single day, 50,000 tons of topsoil blew away. Songwriter and folksinger Woody Guthrie and his wife were living in West Texas at the time of the "Dust Storm Disaster."

"The dust crawled down from the north and the banks pushed the farmers off their land," Woody wrote. "The big flat lakes dried away and left hollow places across the plains full of this hard, dry, crackled, gumbo mud. There isn't a healthier country than West Texas when it wants to be, but when the dust kept whistling down the line blacker and more of it, there was plenty of everything sick, and mad, and mean, and worried." Even music reflected the hard time. A Carter Family song called "No Depression" had the following chorus:

I'm going where there's no depression
To the lovely land that's free from care
I'll leave this world of toil and trouble
My home's in heaven, I'm going there.

West Texans were used to dust storms. The panhandle had long been subject to cycles of rain and drought, so it wasn't unusual to see the wind kicking up small twisters of sandy-colored dirt or to feel the subtle sting of grit in the air. Dust storms visited towns throughout the Great Plains region, Woody recalled. But they were the "blackest and the thickest" along the Texas panhandle. "Just go to Amarillo, Texas, and . . . within walking distance 'round there you'll find you a good dust storm to deal with," he said.

No one knew how long this drought would last. Church congregations prayed for showers, and the town folks analyzed the sky for signs of a good storm, but the dryness held and the dust grew thicker. It penetrated the cracks and crevices of the ramshackle buildings and drizzled across the furniture and dishes. When the wind blew, dust stung the skin and clotted the vision. Because the air was perpetually charged with dirt, people fell victim to a variety of respiratory ailments and began calling them all "dust pneumonia." Most of the time, they joked about it. There wasn't much else they could do. "I've got Texas in my heart, but Oklahoma in my lungs," they'd laugh. But deep down, they grew afraid.

On April 14, 1935, in the middle of the afternoon, the townsfolk noticed the sky darkening over the horizon, as though a tremendous rainstorm were approaching. As they continued to gaze into the distance, however, they realized the black clouds held dust, not rain! As far as they could see, the clouds boiled and boomed, with birds thronging ahead of them, desperate for escape. The temperature began to drop, and the sky grew as dim as dusk, then dark as nightfall. It was a terrifying sight, worse than anything they could have imagined.

"Just to see a thing of that kind a comin' towards you, you wouldn't know exactly what it was," Woody later explained, "'cause it's a freak-looking thing. You never saw anything like it before."

It was a Sunday, he recalled. "A whole bunch of us was standin' just outside of this little town. . . . And so we watched the dust storm come up like the Red Sea closin' in on the Israel children." The people rushed for their houses and storm cellars—if they had them. They shut all their doors and windows, sealing the cracks with towels and old rags, and waited together for what many thought was the end of the world.

"It got so dark you couldn't see your hand before your face," Woody remembered. "You couldn't see anybody in the room." A light bulb "looked just about like a cigarette a burnin'. And that was all the light that you could get out of it."

The clouds swirled with the dark topsoil and clayey earth of the northern Great Plains—hundreds of thousands of tons of it, from as far away as North Dakota. The storm had been traveling toward them for many hours, gaining density and speed as it advanced. By the time it hit Pampa, the wind was gusting at velocities of up to seventy miles an hour, battering the walls and rattling the windows.

Woody and Mary and several other people who had crowded into their shack sat in the cramped living room and waited, most with wet cloths over their mouths to filter out the dust. As they huddled together, listening to the winds and the dirt pounding their little town, they began to discuss their fate. Would the storm ever end?

Or would it destroy everything in its path, including the people of Pampa?

"They just said, 'Well, this is the end. This is the end of the world!'" Woody recalled. "Even the old timers that lived there for fifty years said they never seen anything like it."

Eventually the wall of dust did pass, though the winds raged throughout the night, creating drifts so deep they resembled snow—black snow. By the time the storm ended completely, it had battered the Oklahoma and Texas panhandles along with parts of Kansas, Colorado and New Mexico. It made a lasting impression on Woody. He even wrote a song about it a few years later called "Dust Storm Disaster." From the first verse, the lines were simple, vivid:

On the fourteenth day of April, of 1935,
There struck the worst of dust storms that ever filled the sky.
You could see that dust storm coming,
The cloud looked death-like black.
And through our mighty nation, it left a dreadful track.

The day after the storm, in an article describing the catastrophe, a reporter visiting the region called the storm-ravaged areas a "Dust Bowl." The name was fitting.

At first the townsfolk were excited to be alive, to have survived the devastation of what came to be known as the Great Dust Storm. But after a few days their spirits began to sink. What was happening to the land that had always supported them? The ground refused to yield any crops. The banks refused to loan them money. Their farms were foreclosed and their personal belongings auctioned out from under them to pay their debts—and still they owed. And who knew how long these hard times would last? It seemed a lifetime since any substantial rains had fallen.

For some months—even before the big storm—folks had been packing up their few belongings and leaving town, not just in the Texas panhandle where Woody lived, but in Oklahoma, Kansas, Nebraska, Missouri, Arkansas, Iowa, Colorado and South Dakota—farm states, for the most part. Most of these migrants headed west, and most made the trek by car: Battered wrecks stuffed with families, food and a few odds and ends. They were bound for California, where the valleys were lush and the work plentiful—or so they had heard. They hoped to make a new life, to find a little piece of land and start over.

Woody noticed these travelers and wondered about them. He saw the line of **jalopies**[1] south of town along Highway 66, with flimsy crates and spare tires tied to the roofs and bumpers. Some journeyed on foot, hitching rides when they could. A few straggled into town for gas or provisions. They looked prematurely old, their faces lined and leathery from the wind, their bodies bent from hard labor and disappointment.

Woody had heard rumors about the good life California promised. But for the time being, he was too wrapped up in his music and **impending**[2] fatherhood to wonder too hard about that distant place.

*　*　*

Woody spent money as fast as he earned it, sometimes faster—either that or he gave it away, much to Mary's dismay. In fact, Woody's attitude toward money upset most of the people closest to him, who thought he should be making a real living with a full-time job, especially now that he was married with a baby on the way. Money *was* important to Woody. It was just that he despised it! Oh, he'd admit, it did come in handy

---

[1] **jalopies**—old, run-down cars.

[2] **impending**—approaching; threatening to occur soon.

sometimes. But it also destroyed folks—like his own family, for instance. If his father hadn't been so preoccupied with making money, he might have been around to prevent Clara's fire or Nora's illness[3]—at least that's how Woody saw it. So he promised himself to focus on the important things in life. He was still in the process of discovering exactly what those things were, but he knew one of them was music.

In the fall of 1935, Mary gave birth to a daughter. They named her Gwendolyn Gail but called her "Teeny." Woody marveled over this fragile new life, over her tuft of blond hair, her miniature fingers and toes. Sometimes he sang quiet lullabies to her, and often he bragged about her, but he left the burden of her care to Mary. He began staying out late, sometimes not coming home at all. When he did show up, he passed his time arguing with Mary or sleeping. He was fully aware of his responsibilities as a father, and he rebelled against them, partly because he'd made his own rules for so long, and partly because he was afraid. His daughter seemed so magical, so vulnerable. He was terrified of failing her—so terrified he avoided fatherhood as much as possible. If he had stopped to think about it, he might have spotted the holes in his logic. But as most of his friends and family had already discovered, Woody rarely stopped to think about his choices.

Fatherhood wasn't easy in the 1930s. Even men who wanted to work found it difficult to earn a living. In Pampa, with the oil boom over and the drought hanging on, the number of available jobs continued to shrink. The situation was just about as bad in big industrial cities like Chicago. Factory jobs had dried up, and bills mounted. Families who couldn't pay their debts had their furniture and other belongings repossessed. Many were evicted from their homes, their few remaining

---

[3] Woody's sister, Clara, died in a fire. Woody's mother, Nora, became mentally unstable after Clara's death.

possessions piled on the sidewalks. Men were expected to be tough, to guide their families through hard times. But as the Depression deepened, many found it difficult to stand by and watch their children go without. It was just too painful to bear.

It wasn't easy for the women, either, being pregnant when there was little food to eat, or running a household on **meager**[4]—often nonexistent—budgets. But they were **resourceful:**[5] When the cupboard held only an onion and a bit of potato, they created soup for a family of five. They patched and re-patched their family's clothes, made underwear out of empty flour sacks, went without food so the children could eat, and often looked after relatives who were worse-off than they were.

Woody and Mary were luckier than many folks. From the time they were married until shortly after Teeny's birth, their families lived nearby and tried to help out when they could. But when his marriage to Bettie Jean ended, Charley[6] moved to Arkansas to start over again, and the Jennings family began to grow impatient with their son-in-law. Woody could feel their resentment mounting, and he turned to music for **refuge.**[7]

"I made up new words to old tunes and sung them everywhere I'd go," he wrote. "Some people liked me, hated me, walked with me, walked over me, jeered me, cheered me, rooted me and hooted me. . . . But I decided that songs was a music and a language of all tongues." It brought people together, even people facing devastating losses. For a few hours at a country dance or in a saloon, music could ease a person's troubled mind. Soon Woody was writing verses about the drought,

---

[4] **meager**—thin, sparse.

[5] **resourceful**—able to meet and deal with difficult situations.

[6] Charley was Woody's father. Bettie Jean was Charley's second wife.

[7] **refuge**—shelter or protection from danger or distress.

about the long road to California and all the other images crowding his mind.

"At first it was funny songs of what all's wrong, and how it turned out good or bad," he explained. "Then I got a little brave and made up songs telling what I thought was wrong and how to make it right, songs that said what everybody in that country was thinking."

A number of his early songs described the Great Dust Storm or dust in general. Though he usually borrowed melodies from traditional tunes or hymns, he had a natural flair for writing lyrics. His words were biting and sarcastic, defiant, determined, humorous or corny—often all of these things. But the words were always simple, never **pretentious**.[8] In "Dusty Old Dust" he painted a clear picture:

A dust storm hit, and it hit like thunder;
It dusted us over and it covered us under;
Blocked out the traffic and blocked out the sun.
Straight for home all the people did run.

And through all the verses he weaved a **plaintive**[9] chorus, which sounded even more mournful when he sang it in his unadorned, slightly nasal voice:

So long, it's been good to know you;
So long, it's been good to know you;
So long, it's been good to know you,
This dusty old dust is a gettin' my home,
And I've got to be driftin'along.

---

[8] **pretentious**—showy; making claims to excellence.
[9] **plaintive**—expressive of suffering or woes; melancholy.

QUESTIONS TO CONSIDER

1. How did his music help Guthrie overcome the devastation of the 1935 dust storm?

2. What important role did Guthrie feel that music could play in people's lives during the Depression era?

3. How could money be important to Woody if he despised it?

4. Why does Guthrie compare the dust storm to "the Red Sea closin' in on the Israel children"?

The Dust Bowl

Headlines A huge disaster, the Dust Bowl brought myriads of small tragedies.

DUST DAMAGE

SENDS

MERS FIGHT

STOP LOSSES 'R

DUST STO

IN TWO WEEKS, OR CROP

DUST BOWL WILL BE TOTAL

LOSS, FARM EXPERTS ASSERT

IN SOUTHWES

Storm Brings
fering to Hard
Section

an and Beast Forced
Refuge in Build

This sp

Black Blizzar
of New Mex
Sweeping

ansas, Oklahoma
and Northwes
Ar

LEGISLATION
NECESSARY IN
FIGHTING DUST

ST STORMS RAGE
ROM KANSAS WEST
AR AS CALIFORNIA

Two Pla
As Black

st of Year in 'Nation's Bread Basket
urch Services Halted; Second in Two
Blackens Skies at Guymon, Okla.

Two airplanes w
land at an emergen
miles south of the
port Tuesday afterno
were caught in a
storm that reduced
at the airport

Poster Artist Ben Shahn made this poster for the Resettlement Administration, one of the federal programs designed to bring relief to the thousands touched by the drought.

Liberal, Kansas Five miles away, the dust storm was coming.
▼

Amarillo, Texas   Winds and clouds of dust blew so strong that heavy metal signs waved as if they were flags.

Childress County in the Texas Panhandle   A deserted tenant farmer's cottage gave testimony to the workers who lost their jobs as power tractors replaced them.
▼

Elkharta, Kansas The sky turned black from a huge cloud of dust. ▶

Near Memphis, Texas A family on foot, trundling all they have, moves on.

▼

Cimmaron County, Oklahoma The storm piled dust and sand halfway up this farm outhouse.

Growing Up in the Depression

STUDS TERKEL'S INTERVIEW WITH CESAR CHAVEZ

Cesar Estrada Chavez is famous for the farm workers' union he created in the 1960s. He was born near Yuma, Arizona, in 1927, and grew up in migrant worker camps. In this interview with Studs Terkel, he tells how his family lost its farm, and what life was like "following the crops."

Oh, I remember having to move out of our house. My father had brought in a team of horses and wagon. We had always lived in that house, and we couldn't understand why we were moving out. When we got to the other house, it was a worse house, a poor house. That must have been around 1934. I was about six years old.

It's known as the North Gila Valley, about fifty miles north of Yuma. My dad was being turned out of his small plot of land. He had inherited this from his father, who had homesteaded it. I saw my two, three other uncles also moving out. And for the same reason. The bank had foreclosed on the loan.

If the local bank approved, the Government would guarantee the loan and small farmers like my father would continue in business. It so happened the president of the bank was the guy who most wanted our land. We were surrounded by him: he owned all the land around us. Of course, he wouldn't pass the loan.

One morning a giant tractor came in, like we had never seen before. My daddy used to do all his work with horses. So this huge tractor came in and began to knock down this corral, this small corral where my father kept his horses. We didn't understand why. In the matter of a week, the whole face of the land was changed. Ditches were dug, and it was different. I didn't like it as much.

We all of us climbed into an old Chevy that my dad had. And then we were in California, and **migratory**[1] workers. There were five kids—a small family by those standards. It must have been around '36. I was about eight. Well, it was a strange life. We had been poor, but we knew every night there was a bed *there,* and that *this* was our room. There was a kitchen. It was sort of a settled life, and we had chickens and hogs, eggs and all those things. But that all of a sudden changed. When you're small, you can't figure these things out. You know something's not right and you don't like it, but you don't question it and you don't let that get you down. You sort of just continue to move.

But this had quite an impact on my father. He had been used to owning the land and all of a sudden there was no more land. What I heard . . . what I made out of conversations between my mother and my father—

---

[1] **migratory**—moving from one location to another.

things like, we'll work this season and then we'll get enough money and we'll go and buy a piece of land in Arizona. Things like that. Became like a habit. He never gave up hope that some day he would come back and get a little piece of land.

I can understand very, very well this feeling. These conversations were sort of **melancholy.**[2] I guess my brothers and my sisters could also see this very sad look on my father's face.

That piece of land he wanted . . . ?

No, never. It never happened. He stopped talking about that some years ago. The drive for land, it's a very powerful drive.

When we moved to California, we would work after school. Sometimes we wouldn't go. "Following the crops," we missed much school. Trying to get enough money to stay alive the following winter, the whole family picking apricots, walnuts, prunes. We were pretty new, we had never been migratory workers. We were taken advantage of quite a bit by the labor contractor and the crew pusher.[3] In some pretty silly ways. (Laughs.)

Sometimes we can't help but laugh about it. We trusted everybody that came around. You're traveling in California with all your belongings in your car: it's obvious. Those days we didn't have a trailer. This is bait for the labor contractor. Anywhere we stopped, there was a labor contractor offering all kinds of jobs and good wages, and we were always deceived by them and we always went. Trust them.

Coming into San Jose, not finding—being lied to, that there was work. We had no money at all, and had to live on the outskirts of town under a bridge and dry creek. That wasn't really unbearable. What was

---

[2] **melancholy**—sad, low in spirits.

[3] **crew pusher**—someone who contracts people to do labor for low wages.

unbearable was so many families living just a quarter of a mile. And you know how kids are. They'd bring in those things that really hurt us quite a bit. Most of those kids were middle-class families.

We got hooked on a real scheme once. We were going by Fresno on our way to Delano. We stopped at some service station and this labor contractor saw the car. He offered a lot of money. We went. We worked the first week: the grapes were pretty bad and we couldn't make much. We all stayed off from school in order to make some money. Saturday we were to be paid and we didn't get paid. He came and said the winery hadn't paid him. We'd have money next week. He gave us $10. My dad took the $10 and went to the store and bought $10 worth of groceries. So we worked another week and in the middle of the second week, my father was asking him for his last week's pay, and he had the same excuse. This went on and we'd get $5 or $10 or $7 a week for about four weeks. For the whole family.

So one morning my father made the resolution no more work. If he doesn't pay us, we won't work. We got in a car and went over to see him. The house was empty. He had left. The winery said they had paid him and they showed us where they had paid him. This man had taken it.

Labor strikes were everywhere. We were one of the strikingest families, I guess. My dad didn't like the conditions, and he began to agitate. Some families would follow, and we'd go elsewhere. Sometimes we'd come back. We couldn't find a job elsewhere, so we'd come back. Sort of beg for a job. Employers would know and they would make it very humiliating . . . .

Did these strikes ever win?
Never.

We were among these families who always honored somebody else's grievance. Somebody would have a personal grievance with the employer. He'd say I'm not gonna work for this man. Even though we were working, we'd honor it. We felt we had to. So we'd walk out, too. Because we were prepared to honor those things, we caused many of the things ourselves. If we were picking at a piece rate and we knew they were cheating on the weight, we wouldn't stand for it. So we'd lose the job, and we'd go elsewhere. There were other families like that.

Sometimes when you had to come back, the contractor knew this . . . ?

They knew it, and they rubbed it in quite well. Sort of shameful to come back. We were trapped. We'd have to do it for a few days to get enough money to get enough gas.

One of the experiences I had. We went through Indio, California. Along the highway there were signs in most of the small restaurants that said "White Trade Only." My dad read English, but he didn't really know the meaning. He went in to get some coffee—a pot that he had, to get some coffee for my mother. He asked us not to come in, but we followed him anyway. And this young waitress said, "We don't serve Mexicans here. Get out of here." I was there, and I saw it and heard it. She paid no more attention. I'm sure for the rest of her life she never thought of it again. But every time we thought of it, it hurt us. So we got back in the car and we had a difficult time trying—in fact, we never got the coffee. These are sort of unimportant, but they're . . . you remember 'em very well.

One time there was a little diner across the tracks in Brawley. We used to shine shoes after school. Saturday was a good day. We used to shine shoes for three cents, two cents. Hamburgers were then, as I remember, seven cents. There was this little diner all the way across town. The moment we stepped across the tracks, the police stopped us. They would let us go there, to what we called "the American town," the Anglo town, with a shoe shine box. We went to this little place and we walked in.

There was this young waitress again. With either her boyfriend or someone close, because they were involved in conversation. And there was this familiar sign again, but we paid no attention to it. She looked up at us and she sort of—it wasn't what she said, it was just a gesture. A sort of gesture of total rejection. Her hand, you know, and the way she turned her face away from us. She said: "Wattaya want?" So we told her we'd like to buy two hamburgers. She sort of laughed, a sarcastic sort of laugh. And she said, "Oh, we don't sell to Mexicans. Why don't you go across to Mexican town, you can buy 'em over there." And then she turned around and continued her conversation.

She never knew how much she was hurting us. But it stayed with us.

We'd go to school two days sometimes, a week, two weeks, three weeks at most. This is when we were migrating. We'd come back to our winter base, and if we were lucky, we'd get in a good solid all of January, February, March, April, May. So we had five months out of a possible nine months. We started counting how many schools we'd been to and we counted thirty-seven. Elementary schools. From first to eighth grade. Thirty-seven. We never got a transfer. Friday we didn't tell the teacher or anything. We'd just go home. And they accepted this.

I remember one teacher—I wondered why she was asking so many questions. (In those days anybody asked questions, you became suspicious. Either a cop or a social worker.) She was a young teacher, and she just wanted to know why we were behind. One day she drove into the camp. That was quite an event, because we never had a teacher come over. Never. So it was, you know, a very meaningful day for us.

This I remember. Some people put this out of their minds and forget it. I don't. I don't want to forget it. I don't want it to take the best of me, but I want to be there because this is what happened. This is the truth, you know. History.

QUESTIONS TO CONSIDER

1. Why didn't the government help Chavez's family hold on to its land?

2. What prompted the migrant workers to agitate and strike when the strikes never worked and often cost them their jobs?

3. In what ways was the Depression harder on Mexican-Americans than on white Americans?

Studs Lonigan Looks for a Job

BY JAMES T. FARRELL

Novelist James T. Farrell (1904–1979) wrote about the world that he knew growing up on the South Side of Chicago. His most famous work is a trilogy, a series of three books, about a tough youth, Studs Lonigan, of Irish Catholic descent, like himself. Studs displays the pride, the contempt, the insecurity, and the despair of many who were caught in an unforgiving time. In this excerpt, Studs applies for a job. He has lost money in the stock market. His girlfriend, Catherine, is pregnant and they're getting married in two weeks. And he has had to stop painting houses in his father's construction business because his hard-living lifestyle has already, at 30, weakened his heart. It's the Depression, and jobs are scarce.

Behind a glass-topped desk, set diagonally on a dull, green carpet, Studs saw a thick-browed, full-faced, coldly efficient-looking man whose broad shoulders were covered by the jacket of a black business suit.

He seemed to have the appearance of being fraternity and ex-collegiate, and Studs felt ready to give up.

"Mr. Lonigan, how do you do? I'm Mr. Parker," the man said, arising and extending a large, hairy-backed hand.

"How do you do," Studs mumbled, trying to act like an equal.

"Won't you have a seat?" Mr. Parker said, pointing to the chair at the near side of his desk.

They sat down, and from the corner of his eye Studs glimpsed the wet, dreary **panorama**[1] of Grant Park, the blackened driveways, the gray lake, half-smothered in thick mist.

"Now, what can I do for you, Mr. Lonigan?"

"Well, I thought I would come down to see you about a job," Studs said, and the man's **disconcerting**[2] smile made Studs wish that he was anywhere else but sitting opposite this fellow.

"I don't know if you are aware of it or not, but hundreds come here for that purpose every week."

Studs smiled weakly, feeling that he was giving himself away and showing by his smile that he had no guts, but still he was unable to check it. The man quietly studied him, his penetrating glance making Studs feel even more hopeless.

"How old are you, Mr. Lonigan?"

"I'll be thirty this coming fall," Studs answered, glad for the question because it would lead to talk and break that sitting in silence while that fellow looked through him.

"And how is it that you happen to come to Nation Oil Company? Did somebody send you, or do you know someone already employed here?"

---

[1] **panorama**—a complete view in every direction.

[2] **disconcerting**—in a way that creates discomfort.

"Well, I just thought that it would be a good company to work for," Studs said, hoping that his answer was satisfactory.

Studs felt as if he were a mouse in the hands of a cat while Mr. Parker looked down at his desk, toyed with his pencil. Then with a pointed glance he forced Studs to meet his gaze.

"When did you work last?"

I've been working right along," Studs said, heeding a warning thought not to show his hand or reveal that he desperately needed a job.

"What sort of work have you been doing, Mr. Lonigan?"

"Painting," Studs answered, and the man seemed to raise his eyebrows.

"Artist, you mean?"

"No, house painting," Studs smiled, receiving a return smile which put him more at his ease.

"How does it happen that you want to come to work in a gasoline-filling station? Is it just a lull in your line, and a desire to tide over? Because, you should be informed, when we employ a man, we employ one whom we expect to stay with us and work his way up. Most of our salesmen and many of our executives here, you know, have worked their way up from the service stations. We consider our service stations as a training ground, and hence we cannot employ men just to tide over in dull seasons in their own occupation."

"Well, I'm giving up painting on account of my health, and I got to get a steady job right away. I have to get some other kind of work," Studs said, and, perceiving the frown his remark occasioned, he immediately realized that be had pulled a boner. [3]

"What's the matter with your health, Mr. Lonigan?"

"Well, you know, painting, that is, house-painting, isn't the most healthy occupation in the world. You can

---

[3] boner—blunder.

get lead poisoning, and then, too, my lungs, I've got to watch them and get different work. I'm not in any serious danger, you see, but I just have to change and get some different work. And in changing, I've got to get a good job at outside work, and still something with a future in it."

"Of course, Mr. Lonigan, I trust that you don't consider the Nation Oil Company a health resort," Mr. Parker said after a moment of deep reflection.

"Naturally not," Studs said, not liking the crack,[4] but holding his temper. "I've got to find a job and I'm willing to work hard, as long as there is a chance to get ahead."

He wondered would he have done better by putting all his cards on the table and shooting square. He didn't trust this fellow, but still, if he told more of his story, well, the fellow would have to sympathize with him and give him a break, if there was any break to be given.

"Married?"

"I'm getting married in two weeks."

"How long have you been a painter?"

"Since 1919. I've been working with my father."

"Business bad now?"

"Well, it isn't good. But that's not the reason. I'm leaving because I want to get into something new, and because I got to change my work. You see, on my getting married now, well, I lost two thousand bucks, dollars, that is, on Imbray stock, and then I'm broke, and then, as I said, I got to change my job on account of my health." Studs noticed the **immobile**,[5] cold face before him, and it seemed useless to go on. "Of course, things are not so hot, good, I mean, with my father, and well, under the circumstances, I think I ought to go out and

---

[4] **crack**—witty remark.

[5] **immobile**—fixed, not moving.

work at something for myself. I've been a painter long enough, and now, I'm looking about for a change."

"I see now. At first I wasn't able to understand why you should want to go to a new work that pays less," Mr. Parker said, but still there was that lifelessness in his features.

"And, of course, I'm only asking for a start in a station," Studs said, spurred on to win interest and sympathy. "And I'm sure I can work my way up. I'm not lazy. I've always worked, and I can work."

"What education have you had?"

"Grammar school and some high school."

"Some high school—how much?" Mr. Parker asked **querulously.**[6]

"Two years."

"In Chicago here?"

"Yes, Loyola on the north side," Studs said, and he waited in uncertainty while the man made some jottings on a scratch pad. Maybe he would get it.

"Well, Mr. Lonigan, there isn't really an opening at present. Times are, you know, not the best, and we have only a limited capacity for hiring people. We would like to hire as many as we could, but that, of course, is out of the question. If you and your father have a contract to paint a house, and you hire more men than you need, there isn't any profit. And you say you are how old?"

"I'll be thirty this fall."

"That, also, isn't so good. At thirty a man is still young. But we, you see, like to get our service-station men younger. Just out of college, especially, and train them in our own way. I can't hold out much hope for you, but I'll give you an application blank to fill out and mail in to me, and if there is an opening, I shall get in touch with you."

---

[6] **querulously**—irritably.

"Well, thank you. And, oh, yes, I wanted to say, also, that I can give you good references."

"Of that I don't doubt. I can see that you are an experienced man in your own line and that you have undoubtedly made good at it."

"Well, I can give references like Judge Dennis Gorman, and Mr. McCormack who's high up in the Democratic party."

"Of course, there is no connection between the Nation Oil Company and politics. But then, of course, such references are worthy ones, references of men in public offices, and they will count for you favorably when your application is considered. Now here is an application blank. It is self-explanatory. You fill it out tonight and mail it to me."

"Thanks, I'll do that," Studs said, accepting the blank.

"I'm very glad to have met you, Mr. Lonigan," Mr. Parker said, arising and offering a limp hand.

Studs hurried out past the waiting lineup on the benches. In the corridor, he looked at his watch, eleven-thirty, and pressed the button for an elevator.

QUESTIONS TO CONSIDER

1. Why does Studs feel ready to give up before the interview even starts?

2. Do you think Studs Lonigan will be offered a job at Nation Oil Company? Cite examples from the story that back up your opinion.

from

Dust Tracks on
a Road

BY ZORA NEALE HURSTON

*Zora Neale Hurston (about 1901–1960) was a writer and anthro-
pologist who studied black culture and folklore in the Americas.
Her writings influenced the Harlem Renaissance writers of the
1930s. The following excerpt from her autobiography describes an
incident during the Depression that showed her how principles
can be compromised when a person's ability to make a living is
threatened. She was a university student at the time and was also
working in a barber shop.*

An incident happened that made me realize how
theories go by the board when a person's livelihood is
threatened. A man, a Negro, came into the shop one afternoon and sank down in Banks's chair. Banks was the
manager and had the first chair by the door. It was so
surprising that for a minute Banks just looked at him and
never said a word. Finally, he found his tongue and asked,
"What do you want?"

"Hair-cut and a shave," the man said **belligerently.**[1]

"But you can't get no hair-cut and shave here. Mr. Robins has a fine shop for Negroes on U Street near Fifteenth," Banks told him.

"I know it, but I want one here. The Constitution of the United States—"

But by that time, Banks had him by the arm. Not roughly, but he was helping him out of his chair nevertheless.

"I don't know how to cut your hair," Banks objected. "I trained on straight hair. Nobody in here knows how."

"Oh, don't hand me that stuff!" the crusader snarled. "Don't be such an Uncle Tom."[2]

"Run on, fellow. You can't get waited on in here."

"I'll stay right here until I do. I know my rights. Things like this have got to be broken up. I'll get waited on all right, or sue the place."

"Go ahead and sue," Banks retorted. "Go on uptown, and get your hair cut, man. Don't be so hardheaded for nothing."

"I'm getting waited on right here!"

"You're next, Mr. Powell," Banks said to a waiting customer. "Sorry, mister, but you better go on uptown."

"But I have a right to be waited on wherever I please," the Negro said, and started towards Updyke's chair which was being emptied. Updyke whirled his chair around so that he could not sit down and stepped in front of it. "Don't you touch my chair!" Updyke glared. "Go on about your business."

But instead of going, he made to get into the chair by force.

"Don't argue with him! Throw him out of here!" somebody in the back cried. And in a minute, barbers, customers all lathered and hair half cut, and porters, were all helping to throw the Negro out.

---

[1] **belligerently**—aggressively, with hostility.

[2] Uncle Tom—a black person who wants to earn the approval of whites.

The rush carried him way out into the middle of G Street and flung him down. He tried to lie there and be a **martyr,**[3] but the roar of oncoming cars made him jump up and scurry off. We never heard any more about it. I did not participate in the **mêlée,**[4] but I wanted him thrown out, too. My business was threatened.

It was only that night in bed that I analyzed the whole thing and realized that I was giving sanction to Jim Crow,[5] which theoretically, I was supposed to resist. But here were ten Negro barbers, three porters and two manicurists all stirred up at the threat of our living through loss of **patronage.**[6] Nobody thought it out at the moment. It was an instinctive thing. That was the first time it was called to my attention that self-interest rides over all sorts of lines. I have seen the same thing happen hundreds of times since, and now I understand it. One sees it breaking over racial, national, religious and class lines. Anglo-Saxon against Anglo-Saxon, Jew against Jew, Negro against Negro, and all sorts of combinations of the three. Offhand, you might say that we fifteen Negroes should have felt the racial thing and served him. He was one of us. Perhaps it would have been a beautiful thing if Banks had turned to the shop crowded with customers and announced that this man was going to be served like everybody else even at the risk of losing their patronage, with all of the other employees lined up in the center of the floor shouting, "So say we all!" It would have been a stirring gesture, and made the head-lines for a day. Then we could all have gone home to our unpaid rents and bills and things like that. I could leave school and begin my wanderings again. The "militant" Negro who would have been the cause of it all, would have perched on the smuddled-up wreck of things and

---

[3] **martyr**—one who suffers for the sake of principles.

[4] **mêlée**—a confused struggle.

[5] Jim Crow—laws or rules that discriminate against blacks.

[6] **patronage**—the support of those who buy goods or services from a business.

crowed. Nobody ever found out who or what he was. Perhaps he did what he did on the spur of the moment, not realizing that serving him would have ruined Mr. Robinson, another Negro who had got what he had the hard way. For not only would the G Street shop have been forced to close, but the F Street shop and all of his other six downtown shops. Wrecking George Robinson like that on a "race" angle would have been ironic tragedy. He always helped out any Negro who was trying to do anything progressive as far is he was able. He had no education himself, but he was for it. He would give any Howard University student a job in his shops if they could qualify, even if it was only a few hours a week.

So I do not know what was the ultimate right in this case. I do know how I felt at the time. There is always something fiendish and loathsome about a person who threatens to deprive you of your way of making a living. That is just human-like, I reckon.

QUESTIONS TO CONSIDER

1. Why does the black man accuse Banks of being an "Uncle Tom"?

2. What does Hurston mean when she says that self-interest "rides over all sorts of lines"?

3. In your opinion, did the costs of cutting the black man's hair outweigh the benefits? Explain.

Mary Sweet Organizes African-American Garment Workers

BY DAVID BOYNICK

Because jobs were scarce and there were more people wanting work than could get it, businesses were able to hire workers for pitifully small wages. Union membership grew as people discovered the power of unions to gain higher wages. The interview that follows was conducted by one of the writers working in one of the New Deal Programs, the Federal Writer's Project. In it, Mary Sweet tells of her reasons for being outside the union as well as her experiences as a union organizer.

All workers, white or colored, are hard to organize. They're afraid for their jobs. With the Negro the fear is much greater; it's much harder for them to find jobs. And the union has been dumb in its attitude towards the Negro garment workers in Boston. You see, the important workers in the shops are the cutters and pressers. If you're going to organize a shop you got to get those two. Now, many of the colored girls are pressers and the union simply wouldn't take them in. They weren't prejudiced against our race. It was just that the men in the ILGWU[1] here wanted to keep the pressing jobs for the men, and they kept the union from taking in women pressers. They'd take in the other colored workers, but they couldn't get them. You see, you couldn't tell the colored girls that it wasn't prejudice. I didn't believe that, but almost all of them did. Besides, it wouldn't do 'em much good to get the other girls if they wouldn't organize the pressers.

I lost my job because of the union. In 1933 we had a general strike in Boston. The ILGWU called out everybody, the union and non-union shops. My shop had about half union members. When the strikers came up to my shop to get the workers out, you should have seen the way the union members ducked. They hid under the tables and in the toilet.

They expected I'd go out, but I didn't. My foreman, who was a pretty good union member, said, "Mary, I'm surprised at you." And I said, 'Well you wouldn't take me in the union so I'm independent and I'll do what I want. You gotta take me in before I'll strike." The boss asked if I was afraid and I said no. We had to sneak in and out through the back way. Near the end of the strike he hired thugs to protect us. They finally settled the strike. Our shop signed a union agreement and the women pressers had to get out. They gave us four months to find other jobs.

I loafed for a while and things were tough, real tough. Meanwhile the ILGWU got around to looking at the women pressers the same way that they did in New York and other places; besides, they felt that it was

---

[1] ILGWU—International Ladies Garment Workers Union.

important to organize the colored garment workers of Boston. One day my old foreman came down to see me. He said, "I want you to come with me to talk to some officials of the ILGWU." We went to an Italian restaurant for dinner and they asked me to go to work for the ILGWU as an organizer. They wanted to organize the colored workers, and experience had shown them that it wouldn't be done by white organizers. They had put one white woman on the job as an organizer and then another, and they couldn't get to first place. We talked about it for a while and I said okay. The union sent me to New York and got me a job in a shop and I learned about the union setup and how it worked. I lived while I was there in the home of Mark Starr, the educational director of the ILGWU. He's a fine man and a fine unionist. Then they sent me to Brookwood Labor College for a six-week course, and when that was over I went to Boston and began to work.

It was very discouraging. I sent out a hundred letters for the first meeting I called of colored girls. Six turned out. They told me that wasn't so bad. I kept calling meetings and only a few turned out for each meeting and never the same few. I also went house to house to talk with the girls. Some refused to let me in; some threatened me with knives or said they'd beat me up. One woman in Somerville said, "I'll let you in only because it's freezing out but I'm telling you now that you can talk from now till next week and it won't do no good, my mind is made up." Some said the boss'd told them they didn't need no union.

I worked a little over a year and then the union gave me one week's pay and laid me off. I told them they were making a big mistake, that the only way to organize the colored girls was to stick to it even if it takes years and I knew it would, though they thought it was something that could be done in a few months.

We've got about a hundred in the union today but we're not organizing anymore. I'm an active union member. I work a union shop, but it's really a sweat shop. I guess I average about twenty-five dollars a week. I've got hopes that we may be able to do a lot to make our people union-minded through a Negro Labor Committee such as they have in New York. We've set up such a committee here and I'm the secretary.

The most inspiring thing I ever knew was in New York. A manufacturer, a Jew, ran away from the union and opened up a shop in Harlem. He hired experienced colored girls, and paid them the lowest sweat-shop wages, next to nothing. On the front of the building he put up a sign, "Jesus Saves." He needed an experienced man to cut, so he hired a little Jewish cutter. Before very long the ILGWU organized the girls, about thirty of them, and a strike was called. The Jewish cutter joined the union, too. The strike went on for several weeks and the workers were having a real tough time They were new to the union and flat broke after a few days. But they stuck it out and the boss cracked first. The union and the boss sat down to negotiate and the boss gave in to almost every demand, but one thing he wouldn't do. He wouldn't take the Jewish cutter back to work. He felt that the cutter should have stuck by him because they both were Jewish. Well, they called a meeting of the crew, the thirty girls and the Jewish cutter, and the strikers were told what the boss offered and they were to vote on it. Mind you, they were all dead broke, but they voted unanimously to stay on strike until every one of them was taken back. And they won.

QUESTIONS TO CONSIDER

1. In your opinion, was Mary right to refuse to strike until the union admitted her? Why or why not?

2. Why, after she lost her job, was Mary invited to work for the Garment Workers' Union as an organizer?

3. Why was the Harlem sweat shop strike a major victory for union workers?

Strike!

At a strike-bound Chicago hardware company, 200 police were called in to evict 500 strikers.

Confrontation During the 1934 San Francisco general strike, policemen wielding nightsticks attacked strikers.

▼

A NEW DEAL for CAPITAL LABOR

FOR FULL SOCIAL, ECONOMIC AND. POLITICAL EQUALITY FOR THE NEGRO PEOPLE

UNITE!

AGAINST WAR AND FASCISM

▲
A labor organizer works the docks on New York's waterfront.

◀ **"You can't scare me"** Singing the refrain from a popular union song workers proclaimed, "I'm sticking to the union." Here unemployed workers demonstrated in Columbus, Kansas, in the spring of 1936.

▲

In a railroad yard, a vagrant rests on an empty flatcar bed.

◀ **Nothing to do, nowhere to go.** The signs and the man tell the story of business closings and jobs gone.

The Struggle
for Civil Rights
in the 1930s

BY CLARENCE MITCHELL

Organizations such as the National Association for the Advancement
of Colored People were beginning to make significant progress in
gaining security for the rights of African Americans. In this selec-
tion, Washington Bureau Director Clarence Mitchell recalls the
1930s and his activities with the NAACP. He insists he was nei-
ther brave nor a radical as he covered lynchings for a newspaper
and testified before Congress. Yet his work and that of his
colleagues was pivotal in the history of civil rights in America.

I first became associated with the National
Association for the Advancement of Colored People as a
volunteer in the Baltimore Branch in '32. At that time I
had just finished college and was full of idealism.
Because I was working as a newspaper reporter, the
N A A C P put me in charge of public relations. But the
title I held was really somewhat misleading, because

once you were a member of the local board or in touch with the national officials of the organization, you might be asked to do almost anything: write a useful story or, as in my case, go to public officials to ask their aid in changing conditions. I was asked to participate in efforts to end exclusion of blacks from the police force in Baltimore and to get people into institutions from which they had been excluded on the basis of race. So, while I had the title of public relations director, as a matter of fact I was also involved in the day-to-day operations of the organization.

Fortunately, at that time Walter White, the national executive secretary of the NAACP, struck up a relationship with me and therefore I had an opportunity to have some insight into and impact on the national operations of the organization. It worked this way. Walter would get an idea and he'd want to bounce it off people who were in tune with his approach to things. So he'd ask you to a meeting or, on the other hand, ask you to present some kind of testimony before a legislative body. As a reporter, I had covered a lynching that occurred in Princess Anne, Maryland, in '33, and Walter made sure that I had an opportunity to present that testimony to the Senate Judiciary Committee, which was then holding hearings on an antilynching bill. That was the way he operated; and there were other people in the NAACP, too, who were on the lookout for the young and **volatile**[1] who might have something to contribute to the organization.

As to the lynching, it was something that was well publicized in advance. The victim had been charged with doing something to a white woman. It was never clear what he was charged with, but it turned out it couldn't have been rape. He was arrested on a simple charge of assault and sent from Princess Anne to the

---

[1] **volatile**—light-hearted and lively.

Baltimore city jail, where, supposedly, he would be safe from any mob attack. However, local people on the eastern shore of Maryland who were politically powerful insisted that he be brought back to their jurisdiction, and the governor of the state, who was politically beholden to that group, agreed. It's hard to know why he agreed, since only two years before in Salisbury, in the same area of the state, there had been a lynching, and common sense would have indicated that if there had been a lynching in a larger, hopefully more enlightened community in '31, there was no reason to think there would not be one in '33 in Princess Anne. Nevertheless, the man was brought back and there was a lot of publicity, including indications that he would be lynched. Accordingly, a number of reporters from various papers went to Princess Anne.

No, I wasn't fearful, not because I was brave, but because when you're young you have a lot of illusions, and I had the illusion that the status of a newspaperman was such that it conferred a kind of **immunity**[2] on me. When I got to the town of Princess Anne, I discovered there had in fact been a lynching. The man had been strung up, his body drenched with gasoline and thrown into the middle of the street. The people standing around professed not to know how it had happened. They indicated that a lot of people from Virginia had come and perpetrated this crime, and nobody knew who was responsible. Of course, it later turned out that some of those who were standing around were actually mob members, and there had been a total breakdown of law enforcement. These were the facts I stated in my testimony before the Senate Judiciary Committee.

All I had to do was tell what happened; the events were so horrible in themselves I didn't have to **editorialize**.[3] When you see a fellow human with a rope

---

[2] **immunity**—exemption (as from punishment).

[3] **editorialize**—introduce an opinion when reporting facts.

around his neck and skin coming off his body, you don't need to add any touches of horror.

The most vivid recollection I have of that experience is that while I was waiting to testify, Senator Huey Long, Sr., came to me, and in my dual role as newspaper reporter and witness, it occurred to me that it would be a good story if I could get his opinion of the antilynching legislation. He stood in the doorway of the Senate Caucus Room and, in a loud voice, said, "I don't think much of this bill, but I think some of those senators in there conducting the hearing should be lynched." And he said that at least three times to make sure they would hear.

I think the attitude of the opposition was that whether or not this lynching was the work of people acting outside the law, you couldn't invade the rights of states in order to do anything about it. And, of course, there were others who had stories just as gruesome, so by that time, I think, the country had become a little hardened to what took place in lynchings. People were revolted by it and wanted to do something about it, but the full horror didn't come through, because it wasn't portrayed as **atrocities**[4] would later be on the television screen. We had some horrible pictures of lynchings and yet they could reach only a limited audience, because you had to see them in the papers (and many wouldn't even print them) or at a meeting, where the whole terrible part wouldn't really come through. Still a considerable part of the public was determined to control such things by having a law by which lynchers could be brought to justice.

Unfortunately, there was an equally strong group that felt that lynching was a means of keeping blacks in their place—that if they didn't have such a weapon, blacks, particularly in areas where they were numerically

---

[4] **atrocities**—things that are horrifying, brutal, or cruel.

strong, would take over—and therefore they were attacking the bill. The antilynching law was never passed as a national statute; but the objectives have since been realized in separate statutes. For example, in '60, when we got the Fair Housing Law passed, the Workers' Protection Statute was also passed. But this was really a series of amendments to Title 18 of the criminal code, which gives the government authority to bring criminal prosecutions in almost every conceivable situation where individuals would otherwise have been lynched—for example, if it was a case where a person moved into a neighborhood and the neighbors decided to burn his home and, if he resisted, to lynch him. That is now a criminal offense that can be punished by imprisonment, even life imprisonment, if the victim dies as a result of the crime. So, while the antilynching statute as such was never passed, the basic tools enabling the government to act in these situations did become part of the law.

I think that in some communities where people were comfortable with **segregation,**[5] some of us were considered radicals. I lived in Atlanta for a year during the '30s when I was studying at the School of Social Work. During my stay there, I refused to ride on street-cars and buses because they were segregated, so I walked everywhere. And once, when the oppressive elements in Atlanta attempted to invade an NAACP meeting at which I was present, I verbally attacked them and they finally became **disconcerted**[6] and left. It was such behavior that caused people to think I was a radical.

However, those people were not numerous, because not that many people were well off. I'm pleased to say also that some who *were* well off but had come out of oppressive backgrounds and seen raw violence now wanted to help others. Indeed, a large part of our

---

[5] **segregation**—separation based on race.

[6] **disconcerted**—disturbed, confused.

organization's leadership was made up of people from humble beginnings who had achieved status in business, medicine, and other fields and now were so concerned about segregation that they were willing to lay their lives and properties on the line.

We never had any problems in terms of **credibility.**[7] It's true that during the depression we were under heavy attack from the Communists; but it was their strategy to discredit everybody. They described us as tools of Wall Street, saying that we were not militant enough; but I don't think anybody paid much attention to it. They made several efforts to start organizations to do essentially what the NAACP was doing. They held mass meetings, issued statements and generally beat the drums. But when their ideological and political objectives were found out, they quickly fell apart. So while they got a lot of publicity, they never were a real threat to our organization.

Perhaps the most dramatic illustration of the situation with them was the fight we were making against imposed segregation. Those other groups would have a big demonstration over a statute requiring segregation on intrastate or interstate travel, but they wouldn't raise the money to go to court or get the legislature to change it. By the same token, if a person was charged with a crime and was the source of much newspaper publicity, the group was happy to be involved in it. But once the publicity died down and was no longer suitable for fund-raising, they would bow out. The classic example was the Scottsboro case[8] in '31. Some groups saw a lot of financial possibilities, plus a lot of **ideological**[9]

---

[7] **credibility**—capability of being believed.

[8] Scottsboro case—a legal case in which nine black teenagers were charged with raping two white girls. Despite the lack of evidence, eight of the nine were sentenced to death. Eventually, years later, their sentences were commuted.

[9] **ideological**—pertaining to the theories and doctrines of a political or social program.

opportunities to **exploit,**[10] and used it accordingly. And when those opportunities were exhausted and other issues became more attractive as moneymakers, they got out of the case, whereas the NAACP continued right up to 1977, when we were active trying to get a pardon for the last of the Scottsboro boys. Throughout the years, we had a fund that was used for some of the necessities of the people who had managed to escape or had gotten out of jail and were living in other places. It was discontinued only very recently, and only then because most of the defendants had died or disappeared.

Regarding our efforts against segregation, our strategy was to work under then accepted principles of law to make the separate-but-equal doctrine so obviously incapable of realization that it would fall of its own weight. As a matter of legal requirements, the first and most difficult hurdle was to find a legal theory that would make it clear to the Court that the question raised was not one on which the Court had already made a decision, but on points not ruled on before. Therefore, when we got into the field of education, the point was at the college and professional-school level. We had clear examples of total disregard for the rights of blacks, even with the separate-but-equal theory.

The states' efforts to counter us took various forms. One was that funds were established for blacks to be educated outside the state. Another was to set up regional schools that were segregated. In other words, if you were in Tuskegee, you could set up a school of veterinary training that would be available to blacks in Georgia, Alabama, Tennessee, or wherever. This would mean that blacks who tried to get into a similar school within their own state would be met with the argument that there weren't enough blacks to be in a separate school and therefore they would have to go to the

---

[10] **exploit**—to take advantage of.

regional school. This effort got as far as Congress sanctioning such agreements between the states. In our office, we were able to defeat these resolutions in Congress by showing that the intention was to establish a way of getting around the duty of the state to provide within its borders education to blacks that was equal to that available to whites. And, of course, all the while we knew that there was no way in the world for blacks to be accorded equal education if there were separate institutions. It seemed obvious to us that all we'd have to do is find that there was a certain course in the separate schools, and you were face to face with the conflict of the separate-but-equal doctrine. I remember some humorous observations about very exotic scientific equipment, costing maybe $100,000, being available in one of the white schools. Since obviously they couldn't have two of those, they'd have to admit the blacks.

It wasn't only the colleges where we focused our efforts, but also high schools and other state institutions where blacks were not admitted. There was a public library in Baltimore, for instance, that gave courses to whites in library training. The NAACP challenged successfully, and blacks were admitted to this training program. But our really concentrated, long-term efforts were made at the graduate and professional-school level, because it was believed that this area would be the hardest to even give a semblance of equality on a separate basis. It turned out that this was exactly the case. There was just no way for the states and local political entities to set up anything that was equal, and even when they tried, the courts said they couldn't be equal. This was particularly true in the field of law the courts said, because an important part of the educational process was the interaction between classmates who later would become the prosecutors and judges.

So I would say that as far as state institutions were concerned, our first objective was to get them open.

The trend was based on the Donald Murray case, which challenged the University of Maryland Law School in '35. It was the first case in which a state court struck down the practice of barring blacks on the basis of race. Around '39 there were similar cases in Missouri, Oklahoma and Texas. Later other schools were opened, but even now there is still much to be desired in terms of black enrollment.

I think a by-product of the depression and the suffering in the black community was a greater awareness of what could be done to correct some of the conditions. For example, for years in cities like Chicago, Cleveland and Washington, white owners would open businesses in black neighborhoods with only white people working there. I'm sure had it not been for the depression, people might not have paid much attention to that. But because it was the depression and it was a scramble for jobs, a "buy-where-you-can-work" movement developed in this country, which caused blacks to picket for jobs. And, indeed, one of the famous cases arose in Washington between the New Negro Alliance and the Sanitary Grocery Company. In '38, the Supreme Court upheld the right of blacks to picket in that kind of dispute. Up to that time, a restraining order was issued if blacks picketed in a quest for jobs. Picketing became a very effective movement in almost every community where it was used. It resulted in blacks getting jobs, and in a new look at municipal employment. I remember in Baltimore somebody suddenly realized that blacks couldn't get jobs as street cleaners and as social workers in welfare programs. These also became targets.

Looking back, I feel very encouraged by the fact that it was possible to **surmount**[11] what at that time seemed insurmountable. I do know that what has been

---

[11] **surmount**—to rise above or overcome.

accomplished is permanent only if we fight to preserve it and continue to work to move it forward. It's not the kind of thing that is likely to lull me into a false sense of security. Rather, I think of it as a challenge to know that if one tries, one can succeed.

QUESTIONS TO CONSIDER

1. What were some of the objections to the antilynching legislation proposed by the NAACP?

2. How were the goals of antilynching legislation eventually fulfilled even though the antilynching law was never passed?

3. Why was the NAACP's desegregation strategy effective, particularly in the schools?

4. Based on this article, what do you think was the greatest achievement of the NAACP?

Lorena Hickok to Harry Hopkins

BY LORENA HICKOK

Harry Lloyd Hopkins was head of Roosevelt's Federal Emergency Relief Administration in 1933 and then of the Works Progress Adminstration in 1935. To help him monitor the reponse to these programs, and to balance the professional reports he received from the social workers employed in the programs, he hired Lorena Hickok to give him an intelligent, lay person's view. The following selection includes an excerpt from the introduction to her book of letters to Hopkins and an excerpt from a letter written from Arizona in 1934.

To the "chiselers" and the "shovel-leaners"[1] who have been living on the taxpayers' money these last four years this story is humbly dedicated.

It is their story, as they themselves told it—sometimes desperately, sometimes with quivering lips, sometimes only by the patient, bewildered expression in

---

[1] "chiselers" and the "shovel-leaners"—negative labels given to unemployed people who received money from the government.

their eyes—to one who traveled up and down the country as confidential observer for the man who was charged by their Government with the job of seeing that they did not starve.

Four years ago, to the writer, they were not really people at all. They had no faces. They were just "the unemployed." Muffled figures, backs curved against the wind, selling apples on the street corners of New York. One's friends made jokes about "unemployed apples." Grimy hands thrusting needles and wilting gardenias through your cab window when you were halted in cross-town traffic, while you wondered if you ought to buy them, or if it was "just another racket." Old bundles of rags, presumably soaked in that mixture of water and wood alcohol that the cops called "smoke," sleeping endlessly around rubbish fires along the East river.

"What I want you to do," said Harry Hopkins in July, 1933, "is to go out around the country and look this thing over. I don't want statistics from you. I don't want the social-worker angle. I just want your own reaction, as an ordinary citizen.

"Go talk with preachers and teachers, businessmen, workers, farmers. Go talk with the unemployed, those who are on relief and those who aren't. And when you talk with them don't ever forget that but for the grace of God you, I, any of our friends might be in their shoes. Tell me what you see and hear. All of it. Don't ever pull your punches."

First, a sickening trip on a blistering July morning through Washington's notorious slums, "the Alleys." Then, to Philadelphia. Down into West Virginia and Eastern Kentucky. A month in up-state New York and New England. Two weeks in New York City. Six weeks—and 7,000 miles in an old Chevrolet—in the Dakotas, Nebraska, Iowa, and Minnesota. Down through the Tennessee Valley. Two weeks among the beet sugar workers in Colorado. The Imperial Valley in California, where a thermometer in the car registered 126 degrees Fahrenheit. Fayette county, Pennsylvania, during a coal strike. Aroostook county, Maine, during potato harvest. Bottineau county, North Dakota, just before the first blizzard. Wheeling, West Virginia, when smoke began pouring out of the stacks at the steel mills. Miami, Florida, when the tourists began to come back. Pineville, Kentucky, when relief was cut off. Sioux City, Iowa, when CWA came in. Toledo, Ohio, as WPA was starting. Back and forth, up and down the country. By motor, by train, by plane. A three-year **Odyssey**[2] through every man's land—and no man's land.

One by one, sometimes bold, sometimes hesitant, sometimes demanding, sometimes **faltering,**[3] they emerged—individuals. People, with voices, faces, eyes. People with hope. People without hope. People still fighting. People with all courage squeezed out of them. People with stories.

There was the Negro woman in Philadelphia who used to walk eight miles every day over the scorching pavements just on the chance of getting, perhaps, a little cleaning to do, at 10 cents an hour.

There was the chauffeur in New York who, on the day before he reported for the first time to work as a laborer on a park project, stood about for hours watching how the other men handled their picks and shovels, so he would "get the hang of it and not feel so awkward."

There was the little Mexican girl, aged 6, in Colorado, who said, sure, she'd worked "in the beets" two Summers already and, yes, sometimes she did get pretty tired.

There was the young musician, who said: "For a few weeks it isn't so bad for a man and his wife and baby to

---

[2] **Odyssey**—a long, wandering journey, usually marked by changes of fortune.
[3] **faltering**—wavering, hesitating.

get along on $4.80 a week, paying $3 of it out for rent. But when it runs into months, and you can't see anything ahead, you get damned discouraged."

There was the WPA[4] worker in Erie, Pa., proud as Lucifer because he had developed into "a darned good asphalt man" while working on relief and WPA projects.

There were those unemployed miners' wives in Scotts Run [West Virginia], who instinctively liked and trusted the tall, slender lady with the warming smile and soft, lovely voice who drove up to their homes in an old Ford one Summer day—and found out later that she was the President's wife.

There were those little boys who refused to go to school in Houston, Texas, wearing the trousers of terribly **conspicuous**[5] black-and-white-striped ticking that had been given them, because everybody would know they were on relief.

There were those two small boys, a year or so later, in Salt Lake City, who were overheard boasting about whose father had been on relief longer.

There was the small town woman in Iowa who spent part of her husband's first CWA check for oranges, because she hadn't tasted any for three years.

There was the architect who said he didn't mind working on a road as a day laborer because "at least my children can tell the teacher their father is working. They don't have to say what he's doing."

There was the farm woman in South Dakota who had a recipe for Russian thistle soup and said, "It don't taste so bad, only it ain't very filling."

There was the boy of 20 who limped wearily into his home in a Baltimore suburb one Autumn night in 1934 after having walked nearly 20 miles down into the center of the city and back, "just stopping at every place

---

[4] WPA— The Works Progress Administration was a program initiated by President Roosevelt to stimulate employment.

[5] **conspicuous**—obvious to the eye or mind.

and asking if they didn't need somebody to work—
at anything."

There were those **plucky,**[6] resourceful people in
Lansing, Michigan, who set up a cooperative, issued
scrip to a farmer in return for some vegetables, and,
when the farmer turned it over to an undertaker in part
payment for his wife's funeral, redeemed it by painting
the hearse.

There was that little man with the Charlie Chaplin
mustache and mothy black velour hat set at a patheti-
cally jaunty angle on his grizzly-grey Paderewski
haircut, standing in slush up over his ankles, with his
trousers wet half way to his knees, patiently and clum-
sily pecking away with a shovel he didn't know how to
use, out at Floyd Bennett airport [Brooklyn] one raw
day last February.

There was the former business executive who said:
"It's our wives who resent the pretty young girls they
send out as visitors. Suppose you were my wife—and
I'll bet you are thanking your lucky stars you're not—
run down, without any decent clothes, looking ten years
older than you ought to look. How would you like it if
some smooth-faced young girl, nicely dressed, all made
up, with powder on and lipstick, and pink fingernails,
came into your house, sat down on the edge of a chair,
and began to ask you a lot of personal questions?
You'd want to throw something at her, wouldn't you?
The contrast is just too painful, that's all. Couldn't
they send middle-aged men, maybe? Then the neighbors might not guess, either. They might think they
were just peddlers."

There was the unemployed fur-worker in Pittsburgh
who said: "Lady, you just can't know what it's like to
have to move your family out of the nice house you had
in the suburbs, part paid for, down into an apartment,

---

[6] **plucky**—having courage or spirit.

down into another apartment, smaller and in a worse neighborhood, down, down, down, until finally you end up in the slums."

There was that woman in her late thirties, with the thin, sensitive face, in Bakersfield, California, who said timidly: "I can talk to you about this now, because we aren't on relief any more. It's this thing of having babies. You've got no protection at all. You don't have any money, you see, to buy anything at the drugstore. And there you are, surrounded by young ones you can't support. And always afraid. All you have is a grocery order. I've known women to try to sell some of their groceries to get a little money to buy the things they need at the drugstore. But if they catch you at it, they take you off relief. Maybe they wouldn't if they really knew what you wanted the money for, but most women don't like to talk about those things to outsiders. You understand, don't you? I'm not asking for anything for myself. My husband is working now. We're not on relief any more. I suppose you can say the easiest way would be not to do it. But it wouldn't be. You don't know what it's like when your husband is out of work. He's gloomy all the time and unhappy. You haven't any money for movies, or anything to take his mind off his troubles. You must try all the time to keep him from going crazy. And many times—well, that is the only way."

One by one, they come and go. Not all of them saints, by any means. And not all of them, by any means, dishonest or lazy or hopeless. Thousands of them in the last three years have "come back," have found jobs as industry revived, have moved out of the crowded flats where they were living with relatives, have paid up their debts. Perhaps—and it is to be hoped that this is so—many of them have even forgotten that there ever was a Depression! And thousands of them have not found jobs, perhaps never will. A reviving industry, with the best of intentions, cannot immediately absorb such a load as piled up in this country during the black years. The young, the physically fit, the mentally alert first are called and should be. The man over 40, the untrained, the weak, for many of these there may be no future at all. They must remain, to the ends of their lives, in the ranks of the tattered legion of the economically damned.

"Chiselers" and "shovel-leaners" who have been living on the taxpayers' money these last four years—this is their story. And to them it is dedicated, in all sincerity and humility.

To Harry L. Hopkins
Phoenix, Arizona, May 4, 1934

Dear Mr. Hopkins:

. . . I have been writing you right along that the only way I could see to clean up this Negro-Mexican business would be to reinvestigate thoroughly the Negro and Mexican case loads, closing the intakes to get them out of the habit of registering for relief for a few weeks and to turn the case workers loose for the reinvestigation, and to force every Negro or Mexican who could get any work at all, at W H A T E V E R wages, to take it and get off the relief rolls. I must admit that there are people in the set-up who don't agree with me on this. They argue first of all that we are forcing these people into **peonage.**[7] Employers, particularly farmers and housewives—the two worst classes of employers in the country, I believe—will take advantage of the situation. I've written you about housewives who think Negroes, Mexicans, or even white girls ought to be glad to work for their room and board. And last week in New Mexico

---

[7] **peonage**—a position of being unable to get ahead as a result of working at a low-wage job.

I heard about sheep growers who want to hire herders at $7 a MONTH! It is also argued that, particularly in cities, thousands of the Mexicans and Negroes actually CAN'T get work—that, if there is any job, no matter how lowly and how poorly paid, a white man will take it, and that there would be Hell to pay if a Negro or a Mexican got it. I don't believe that, however, to the extent that some people do.

It's almost impossible to get to the bottom on this farm labor proposition. The farmers—sheep and cattle men, cotton growers, and so on—are all yelling that they can't get the Mexicans to work because they are all on relief. But when Mexicans and Spanish-Americans won't go out and herd sheep for $7 a month because they can get $8 or $10 on relief, it seems to me that the farmer ought to raise his wages a little. Oh, they don't admit trying to get herders for $7 a month. If you ask them what they are paying, they will say, "Anywhere from $15 a month up." But our relief people looked into the matter and found out what they actually were willing to pay.

A thing that complicates the whole situation right now is our hourly rate under the new program. In Arizona, for instance, the minimum is 50 cents an hour. We adopted it because it is the hourly rate on public works in the state of Arizona. But, don't you see, it's a "political" hourly rate? Jobs on highways on public works in Arizona are dealt out as political patronage. The ACTUAL prevailing wage in Arizona is nowhere nearly that high. Up to now there haven't been many people getting 50 cents an hour in Arizona—and damned few Mexicans. Now we come along and announce we are going to pay everybody on relief 50 cents an hour. You can imagine the furor.

QUESTIONS TO CONSIDER

1. How did the author's opinion of the unemployed change after her three-year road trip as a confidential observer?

2. Why does the author consider her subjects the unsung heroes of the Depression?

3. Why were many of the people on welfare unable to find work after the Depression?

4. Do you agree with the author's solution for reducing the number of Mexicans and Negroes on welfare? Why or why not?

Food Relief

For many men without work, soup kitchens provided a hot meal.

Capone's Kitchen In an effort to improve his image, Al Capone opened a soup kitchen in Chicago.

This line of men wait for "free soup, coffee, and doughnuts for the unemployed" outside Capone's soup kitchen in 1931.
▼

Apples for Sale Right by the steps of the Capitol, an unemployed man sells apples to passersby for five cents each.

Bread Line The extent of unemployment during these years can be seen in this picture of a bread line beside the Brooklyn Bridge.
▼

Eleanor Roosevelt The President's wife went everywhere, sharing in private as well as public efforts to relieve suffering. Here she ladles soup from a large kettle in a soup kitchen.

Excerpts from the Diary of Eleanor Roosevelt

BY ELEANOR ROOSEVELT

In her public life, Eleanor Roosevelt was a tireless advocate for human rights. During the Depression she traveled the country observing social conditions and helping to shape New Deal policy. Later, from 1945–1953, she was the United States representative to the United Nations and chaired the committee that wrote the Universal Declaration of Human Rights. Throughout most of her life she kept a diary in which she recorded her private thoughts. Here, her personal philosophy unfolds from day to day as she reflects on events. These four excerpts come from the diary for 1936.

"A Fish Bowl"

Washington, January 7—Someone sent me a most amusing present. When I came into my room this afternoon, I thought I was being visited by a zoo, for it was surrounded by four polar bears. On closer inspection, however, I found that the polar bears were guarding a goldfish bowl, with three lovely lilies growing out of the center and a red rose floating to the surface and the goldfish swimming around.

The donor had a sense of humor, for to me a goldfish bowl is certainly suggestive. I doubt if anyone living in the White House needs such a constant reminder, for whether they write themselves, or just trust those who write about them, no goldfish could have less privacy from the point of view of the daily happenings of their existence.

There is, however, one **consolation**[1] to anyone who lives in the public eye, namely, that while it may be most difficult to keep the world from knowing where you dine and what you eat and what you wear, so much interest is focused on these somewhat unimportant things that you are really left completely free to live your own inner life as you wish.

Thank God, few people are so poor that they do not have an inner life which feeds the real springs of thought and action. So, if I may offer a thought in consolation to others who for a time have to live in a "goldfish bowl," it is: "Don't worry because people know all that you do, for the really important things about anyone are what they are and what they think and feel, and the more you live in a 'goldfish bowl' the less people really know about you!"

"Fascism, Communism, and Democracy"

Hyde Park, April 27—I have been thinking a great deal about the peace meetings which young people held all over the country on April 22nd. From the letters I receive and from the talks which I have had, there is no question in my mind that young people are definitely

---

[1] **consolation**—the act of consoling or comforting.

determined to do away with war, but they really are very indefinite as to the way in which it shall be done.

I often wonder if they realize that every new form of government, fascism, communism, or our own democracy, originally had for its purpose the making of a world in which people could be happy and content. As individuals, people felt helpless to accomplish their desires and so, in different places, they were led to believe, by various types of people, that these desires could be accomplished in different ways.

To me the real strength of the democratic theory, in opposition to fascism or communism, is that fascism frankly states certain people will tell other people what they shall do to be happy and those people have nothing or little to say about it.

In theory the Communists are to do everything in common, in practice a small group also tells other people what they shall do to achieve their objectives. So far, more nearly than any other form of government, the democratic form has allowed people to shape their own government. While more important leaders have arisen here and there, still, on the whole, the controls have been kept in the hands of the majority of the people.

If these young people are really going to get any-where, they must realize that **inveighing**[2] against a thing is all very well, but their future success lies in controlling democracy. Only if democracy makes individuals better able to attain their ideals will it survive the test of today.

What the young people must do is to find out how their government can meet the demands of the people. Find out how business and invention and what we call modern civilization can bring a greater degree of freedom from fear of any kind, and therefore a greater degree of happiness to the average individual.

---

[2] **inveighing**—protesting or complaining bitterly.

"Duty"

Hyde Park, July 13—This afternoon I went to see a very lovely friend of mine, and when I was about to leave she remarked: "I think in this life we always have to do our duty."

I gasped for a moment, for that sentiment goes back to my grandmother's day at least. It is far more typical of our New England ancestors than the average philosophy of today. Must we always do our duty? If so, how are we always to know what is our duty?

A wise aunt of mine used to say: "Do anything you want to do, but always be quite sure that in your heart of hearts you are at peace with yourself about doing it. It does not matter what people think, but if you are uncomfortable yourself then you will have no happiness."

I believe that I would rather like to go through life with this more cheerful philosophy of trying to make duty coincide as far as possible with what one would like to do, being sure, however, that what I do leaves my inner consciousness satisfied and untroubled.

"Proppers and Propped"

Hyde Park, August 7—At the county League of Women Voters' meeting yesterday, I was talking with a group of ladies when I saw an elderly woman painfully get out of a car and, with the aid of a cane, walk up the short driveway and climb the rather steep hill to the house. I thought it remarkable that anyone so lame should come to the meeting. The much-used car that had left her drove away.

My hostess murmured an Italian name to me and the old lady was thrust into a chair in front of me. Holding my hand in both of hers, she uttered a stream of Italian words. I tried unsuccessfully to talk with her in English. But her face lit up when I spoke a few words in Italian.

Still thinking she had come solely for the meeting, I moved over to chat with another group and was quite surprised when she hobbled toward me, shook my hand, said something about her rheumatism, turned around and, with two others helping her, proceeded **laboriously**[3] down the steps and the hill. No car was in sight.

I inquired where she lived. They said her home was up a side road, about a mile away. I realized it would be agony for her to walk that distance, so I asked her to wait while I got my car. With some difficulty I helped her in and we started for her home.

She talked rapidly in Italian and I gathered that she lived with a son and his wife and several children; that hard as life was, it was easier than it had been, and she said a prayer for the President every night. That was why she had come to the meeting—just to tell me that she prayed for him!

Arriving at the house, on a very bad road, I found four grown persons—two of them very old—and six children, one only a baby. The oldest boy attended high school and was the pride of the family, because of four prizes won this year, with the possibility of a scholarship.

The family came from the Bronx, in New York City, a year ago, off relief and accepted for resettlement. They are running a small poultry farm. Their great happiness is that the children are being educated, are healthier and now have enough to eat. In fact, the "living is good," but the payments to the government are hard to meet.

I chatted a while and wondered if, in their place, I could make payments either, with ten mouths to feed. I shall follow this family's fortunes with interest from now on.

As I read in bed last night I came upon the following: "The human race is divided into the proppers and

---

[3] **laboriously**—industriously; with tedious effort.

the propped. The propped have an easier time, of course, but they do not live so deeply or so excitingly and they get bored."

I put the book down and chuckled as I fell asleep.

QUESTIONS TO CONSIDER

1. To Mrs. Roosevelt, what view of human nature does the goldfish bowl reflect?

2. What do you think of Mrs. Roosevelt's response to her friend's position on doing one's duty?

3. Why is Mrs. Roosevelt critical of the young people who have protested against war?

4. Why do you think Mrs. Roosevelt chuckles after reading the passage about the "proppers" and the "propped"?

End of the Depression

BY PIRI THOMAS

In the following excerpt from his autobiographical novel, Down
These Mean Streets, *Puerto-Rican American author Piri Thomas
describes how the Depression ended for his family. Most historians
agree that it was the advent of the World War II that brought the
Great Depression to an end, not only in America, but throughout
the world.*

It was 1941, and the Great Hunger called Depression
was still down on Harlem. But there was still the good
old WPA.[1] If a man was poor enough, he could dig
a ditch for the government. Now Poppa was poor
enough again.

The weather turned cold one more time, and so did
our apartment. In the summer the cooped-up apartments in Harlem seem to catch all the heat and improve

---

[1] WPA— The Works Progress Administration was a program initiated by
President Roosevelt to stimulate employment.

on it. It's the same in the winter. The cold, plastered walls embrace that cold from outside and make it a part of the apartment, till you don't know whether it's better to freeze out in the snow or by the stove, where four jets, wide open, spout **futile**,[2] blue-yellow flames. It's hard on the rats, too.

Snow was falling. "My *Cristo*," Momma said, *"qué frio*.[3] Doesn't that landlord have any *corazón*?[4] Why don't he give more heat?" I wondered how Pops was making out working a pick and shovel in that falling snow.

Momma picked up a hammer and began to beat the beat-up radiator that's copped a plea from so many beatings. Poor steam radiator, how could it give out heat when it was freezing itself? The hollow sounds Momma beat out of it brought echoes from other freezing people in the building. Everybody picked up the beat and it seemed a crazy, good idea. If everybody took turns beating on the radiators, everybody could keep warm from the exercise. . . .

The door opened and put an end to the kitchen yak. It was Poppa coming home from work. He came into the kitchen and brought all the cold with him. Poor Poppa, he looked so lost in the clothes he had on. A jacket and coat, sweaters on top of sweaters, two pairs of long johns, two pairs of pants, two pairs of socks, and a woolen cap. And under all that he was cold. His eyes were cold; his ears were red with pain. He took off his gloves and his fingers were stiff with cold.

"Cómo está?"[5] said Momma. "I will make you coffee."

Poppa said nothing. His eyes were running hot frozen tears. He worked his fingers and rubbed his ears,

---

[2] **futile**—useless.

[3] *qué frio*—how cold!

[4] *corazón*—heart.

[5] *Cómo está?*—How are you?

and the pain made him make faces. "Get me some snow, Piri," he said finally.

I ran to the window, opened it, and scraped all the snow on the sill into one big snowball and brought it to him. We all watched in frozen wonder as Poppa took that snow and rubbed it on his ears and hands.

"Gee, Pops, don't it hurt?" I asked.

"*Sí*, but it's good for it. It hurts a little first, but it's good for the frozen parts."

I wondered why.

"How was it today?" Momma asked.

"Cold. My God, ice cold."

Gee, I thought, *I'm sorry for you, Pops. You gotta suffer like this.*

"It was not always like this," my father said to the cold walls. "It's all the fault of the damn depression."

"Don't say 'damn,'" Momma said.

"Lola, I say 'damn' because that's what it is—*damn.*"

And Momma kept quiet. She knew it was "damn."

My father kept talking to the walls. Some of the words came out loud, others stayed inside. I caught the inside ones—the damn WPA, the damn depression, the damn home relief, the damn poorness, the damn cold, the damn crummy apartments, the damn look on his damn kids, living so damn damned and his not being able to do a damn thing about it. . . .

The next day the Japanese bombed Pearl Harbor.

"My God," said Poppa. "We're at war."

"*Dios mío*," said Momma.

I turned to James. "Can you beat that?" I said.

"Yeah," he nodded. "What's it mean?"

"What's it mean?" I said. "You gotta ask, dopey? It means a rumble[6] is on, and a big one, too."

---

[6] rumble—a slang term used to describe a fight, usually between gangs.

I wondered if the war was gonna make things worse than they were for us. But it didn't. A few weeks later Poppa got a job in an airplane factory. "How about that?" he said happily. "Things are looking up for us."

Things *were* looking up for us, but it had taken a damn war to do it. A lousy rumble had to get called so we could start to live better. . . .

I couldn't figure it out, and after a while I stopped thinking about it. Life in the streets didn't change much. . . . War or peace—what difference did it really make?

QUESTIONS TO CONSIDER

1. The WPA (Works Progress Administration) was hailed by many as a brilliant solution to unemployment. Why, then, does Piri's father damn the WPA?

2. What good did it do to beat the radiators on the cold days?

3. Ironically, how was Piri's family—and many families like his—saved by World War II?

Documenting the Depression

Russell Lee

Shacktowns Russell Lee worked for the Farm Security Administration to record the depression years. Here is his photograph of migrant workers who lived in makeshift homes called "shacktowns," like this one in Oklahoma City.

▲

F.S.A. Camps Here the family of a farm worker in Friendly Corners, Arizona, is shown in their mobile home provided by the Farm Security Administration (F. S. A.).

Living in Tents Many children grew up living in makeshift tents like this one in Harlingen, Texas. ▶

Agricultural Camps Migrants who worked on farms gathered together in camps. At this one—called May's Avenue Camp—Lee photographed a family of six in front of their home in July of 1939.

The Elmer Thomas family of migrants leaves their home for California.
▼

Household Equipment Here another child of a migrant family in Harlingen, Texas, stands in front of the household stove and washstand.
▼

Dorothea Lange

Documenting an Era Another Depression photographer commissioned by the F.S.A., Dorothea Lange is probably the most recognizable person to document the era of the Depression on film. Here is Lange's photo of an eighteen-year-old migrant mother and her daughter outside their tent home.

Traveling Lange's photographs of the Depression have a poignance rarely matched by other photographers. Here an Arkansas family of nine is traveling cross-country in an effort to find work in the California harvests. ▶

Migrant Family Here Lange captures a family traveling between Dallas and Austin, Texas, in August of 1936.

ACKNOWLEDGEMENTS

10 "Depressions are Farm Led and Farm Fed" from *Hard Times: An Oral History of the Great Depression* by Studs Terkel. Copyright © 1970 by Studs Terkel. Reprinted by permission of Pantheon Books, a division of Random House, Inc.

14 "Investments Soared" from *From the Crash to the Blitz* 1929-1939 by Cabell Phillips. Copyright © 1969 by *The New York Times*. Reprinted by permission.

19 "October 24, 1929" from *A Nation in Torment* by Edward Robb Ellis. Copyright © 1970 by Edward Rob Ellis.

30 "Ed Uhl, Bank Loan Officer, and Marty Ducceschi, Depositor" from *The Day America Crashed* by Tom Shachtman. Copyright © 1979 by Tom Shachtman.

36 "What Caused the Crash?" from *A Nation in Torment* by Edward Robb Ellis. Copyright © 1970 by Edward Rob Ellis.

48 "Brother, Can You Spare a Dime?" by E. Y. Harburg and Jay Gornay. © 1932 (Renewed) Warner Bros. Inc. Rights for Extended Renewal Term in United States controlled by Glocca Morra Music and Gorney Music Publishers. Canadian Rights controlled by Warner Bros. Inc. All rights reserved. Used by Permission. WARNER BROS. PUBLICATIONS U.S. INC., Miami, FL 33014

50 "Interview with E.Y. (Yip) Harburg" from *Hard Times: An Oral History of the Great Depression* by Studs Terkel. Copyright © 1970 by Studs Terkel. Reprinted by permission of Pantheon Books, a division of Random House, Inc.

54 "Bonus Army March on Washington" by John Dos Passos. From *Brother, Can You Spare a Dime?* by Milton Meltzer. Copyright © 1969 by Milton Meltzer. Reprinted by permission of Alfred A. Knopf, Inc.

61 "President Hoover's Efforts" from *The Great Depression*, copyright © 1986 by John Garraty, reprinted by permission of Harcourt Brace & Company.

70 "The Biggest Thing Except for Wars" by J. Douglas Brown. Reprinted from *Decade of Destiny* by Judah and Alice Graubart, © 1978. Used with permission of NTC/Contemporary Publishing Group, Inc.

73 "Red Cross Relief . . . for Who?" by Will Rogers. From *Brother, Can You Spare a Dime?* by Milton Meltzer. Copyright © 1969 by Milton Meltzer. Reprinted by permission of Alfred A. Knopf, Inc.

83 "The First One Hundred Days" from *From the Crash to the Blitz 1929-1939* by Cabell Phillips. Copyright © 1969 by *The New York Times*. Reprinted by permission.

114 "The Dust Bowl" from *Woody Guthrie: American Balladeer* by Janelle Yates. Courtesy of Ward Hill Press.

130 "Growing Up in the Depression" from *Hard Times: An Oral History of the Great Depression* by Studs Terkel. Copyright © 1970 by Studs Terkel. Reprinted by permission of Pantheon Books, a division of Random House, Inc.

137 "Studs Lonigan Looks for a Job" from *Studs Lonigan: A Trilogy* by James T. Farrell. Reprinted by permission of International Creative Management, Inc. Copyright © 1932 James. T. Farrell.

143 From *Dust Tracks on a Road* by Zora Neale Hurston. Copyright 1942 by Zora Neale Hurston. Copyright renewed 1970 by John C. Hurston. Reprinted by permission of HarperCollins Publishers, Inc.

147 "Mary Sweet Organizes African-American Garment Workers" by David Boynick. From *First Person America* by Ann Banks. *First Person America* was published in paperback by W. W. Norton. Reprinted by permission of the author.

158 "The Struggle for Civil Rights in the 1930s" by Clarence Mitchell. Reprinted from *Decade of Destiny* by Judah and Alice Graubart, © 1978. Used with permission of NTC/Contemporary Publishing Group, Inc.

183 Excerpts from *Eleanor Roosevelt's My Day* edited by Rochelle Chadakoff. Reprinted by permission of United Feature Syndicate, Inc.

189 "End of the Depression" from *Down These Mean Streets* by Piri Thomas. Copyright © 1967 by Piri Thomas. Reprinted by permission of Alfred A. Knopf, Inc.

Every effort has been made to secure complete rights and permissions for each selection presented herein. Updated acknowledgements, if needed, will appear in subsequent printings.

Photo Research Diane Hamilton

Photos courtesy of the Library of Congress and the National Archives in Washington, D.C.

Index